110

Femi

A Beginner's Guide

ONEWORLD BEGINNER'S GUIDES combine an original, inventive, and engaging approach with expert analysis on subjects ranging from art and history to religion and politics, and everything in between. Innovative and affordable, books in the series are perfect for anyone curious about the way the world works and the big ideas of our time.

Beginners
GUIDES

Feminism
A Beginner's Guide

Sally J. Scholz

ONEWORLD

OXFORD

A Oneworld Book

Published by Oneworld Publications 2010

Copyright © Sally J. Scholz 2010

The right of Sally J. Scholz to be identified as the
Author of this work has been asserted by her in
accordance with the Copyright, Designs and Patents Act 1988

ISBN 978–1–85168–712–1

Typeset by Jayvee, Trivandrum, India
Cover design by vaguelymemorable.com
Printed and bound in Great Britain by TJ International, Padstow

Oneworld Publications
UK: 185 Banbury Road, Oxford, OX2 7AR, England
USA: 38 Greene Street, 4th Floor, New York, NY 10013, USA
www.oneworld-publications.com

For Jane

*My sister and I, you will recollect, were twins,
and you know how subtle are the links
which bind two souls which are so closely allied.*

Arthur Conan Doyle,
The Adventure of the Speckled Band

Contents

Acknowledgments

There are so many wonderful feminist mentors in my life and I am deeply grateful for the paths they paved and the struggles they won. Thank you! Thanks also to all of the students who took 'Philosophy of Women,' 'Feminist Epistemologies,' 'Feminist Theories,' 'Seminar on Simone de Beauvoir,' and 'Race, Class, Gender' with me at Villanova University. No doubt they will recognize some of my well-worn expressions in the pages of this book.

Thanks also to the editors at Oneworld, Marsha Filion and Fiona Slater for their patience, advice, and good humor.

Most especially, I want to express my gratitude to Jane LePage. Jane gave me the prodding and encouragement I needed to complete this text; she read every word and offered excellent advice for revising the manuscript. I truly could not have completed this project without her.

I am extremely grateful to my family, my husband Christopher Kilby and our children Tessa Scholz Kilby and Luke Scholz Kilby, for their love, patience, and joy. Tessa and Luke teach me about the future of feminism each and every day.

1

What is feminism?

What *is* feminism? *Who* is a feminist?

One thing is for sure, there is no membership card or pledge of allegiance to the cause, there is no litmus test or any sort of test actually. Perhaps we might answer that to be a feminist one merely has to claim it as an identity. But 'identity' is itself a troubling word. If I say I am a feminist does that mean that everything I do will be *as* a feminist? Does it mean that I have to dress, act, and speak like others who also say they are feminists? Do I have to follow a feminist dogma? And what about this notion of an individual *claiming* an identity? What could that mean and do all individuals have the freedom and power to do such claiming? For that matter, why would we want to say being a feminist is merely a choice for an *individual?* Clearly, there is a lot to think about regarding these terms 'feminism' and 'feminist.'

The most common and perhaps most general understanding of feminism is that feminism is about equal rights for women. As general understandings go, this one rates only 'ok.' Feminism *is* about equal rights for women but what that means is much more complicated than it appears at first blush. Moreover, feminism isn't *just* about equal rights for women. *Feminism is a critical project.* It looks at all aspects of life to identify those elements that might be oppressive and suggests alternatives. By 'critical' I do not mean that feminism rejects anything that it does not like. Rather critical means that there is an inquiry into the message and values of something. Criticism is an activity that seeks to analyze and understand something – a practice, a custom, a language, a social role. In seeking to understand, however, criticism also asks what values and presuppositions are being implied by the thing. A critical look at the world would dissect it into various parts – language, laws, social roles, practices, for instance – and seek to uncover what else is being suggested beyond the mere facts. A feminist reading, as a critical project, would look especially at what is being said about women: what social roles are they expected to take, what are their liberties or privileges in relation to men, and similar sorts of inquiries. In addition, if the feminist has specific interests or concerns, then she or he might emphasize particular aspects of the critical project. Feminists glimpse the world through a different lens and what they see usually requires a response. Feminism, in other words, follows the critical project with action to bring about social change.

Feminist methodologies

Many types of feminism abound and they take their motivations and inspirations from different sources. Nonetheless, there are some feminist methodologies that, while not universal to all feminisms, might be helpful to discuss as a way to answer that initial question: what is feminism?

There is an important difference between feminist theory as a subfield of an academic discipline such as philosophy and feminist theory as a methodology. According to the former, there are topics and issues within the discipline which are 'feminist' and others which are not. As a methodology, on the other hand, feminist theory is a way of doing the discipline that may be applicable in every subfield within that discipline. There is feminist literature, feminist economics, feminist history, feminist sociology, feminist psychology, and so on. For our purposes, I will use the term 'feminist methodology' as a sort of umbrella concept to indicate a feminist way of doing something.

When you hear the word 'feminist' take a step back and look at the context. Ask what the project is and 'what makes this feminist?' 'Feminist' might mean a movement for social change or it might mean a concern for all forms of oppression. It definitely has a critical edge to it and there is an end or goal for which it strives. Feminism cannot be a field of study like ancient Greek, which can be studied without social and political effects. Rather, feminism aims at liberation and that makes it political. To read feminist literature, to write feminist theory, to engage in feminist praxis is to participate in some process for personal and social transformation. Even if one vehemently disagrees with what is being read, argued, or done, one participates in that critical project to think about assumptions, structures, values, and activities in a new way – a way that is meant to challenge.

Feminist methodology takes the lives of women as central.

First, making the lives of women the starting point for theory and practice might mean addressing the ways women have been excluded either intentionally or unintentionally. For example, Immanuel Kant's moral theory is based on duty. An action is morally right if and only if it accords with duty. But Kant also says that women are incapable of duty. Clearly, this is an example of women being explicitly and perhaps intentionally excluded by a normative moral theory. At other times, the exclusion is not so explicit but is somehow built into the very structure of the theory itself. In practice, the exclusion can also be explicit or hidden. An example of women being explicitly excluded from social life may be found in Afghanistan under Taliban rule. Women were not allowed to be outside without a male relative and even then had to be covered from head to foot in the burka.

Next, looking at the lives of women as a starting point for thinking about and acting as a feminist means focusing in on women's vast and diverse experiences of oppression to see how those experiences challenge theory and practice. For instance,

Scholars and activists look at the social, civic or political, material, psychological, and embodied elements of women's existence. By scrutinizing the resource allocation and political power of women compared to men, feminists identify and reveal the complex patterns of social arrangement that detrimentally impact women. For instance, feminists do all of the following in various ways and at various times:

- Ask if women are unequal, how they are unequal, and why;
- Identify forms of violence against women;
- Examine connections between forms of oppression;
- Focus on issues affecting women;
- Apply insights garnered from the experiences of women to scrutinize resource allocation, theory, cultural presentation, etc.
- Critique the cultural, philosophical, and political tradition (though they do not necessarily reject these traditions).

learning about how rape affects a woman likely changes how criminal courts understand reasonableness and responsibility.

Finally, taking women's lives as central means articulating and validating insight that comes from women, whether based on women's status as oppressed, based on women's unique social roles and experiences, or, according to some feminists, based on some inherent or essential characteristic of what it means to be women. Feminist theory often uses narratives and histories to challenge and improve existing theories or to propose new ones. Feminist activism tries to bring about social change that will value women's contributions to culture.

The idea is not to offer a definitive explanation of feminist methodology but rather to provide a way of thinking about the wide varieties of feminist concerns and begin to explore what they have in common, what they have to offer, and how they all get placed under the broad heading of feminism. One way to think about the varying methodologies within feminist theories is to understand that feminist theorists are usually engaged in (1) critiquing the status quo, the canon, or traditional theory; or (2) constructing new theory built on the insights gained from critique and/or the insights obtained from taking the lives of women as central to theorizing; or (3) reflective dialogue regarding their own or other feminist theory. Of course, sometimes, these tasks are undertaken simultaneously or in tandem.

Waves of feminist thought and action

The United States revolution and the French revolution in the eighteenth century brought about an interest in liberty that extended beyond the anti-colonialist interests of the Americans or the anti-bourgeoisie sentiments of the French revolutionaries. Although interest in (and struggles for) the rights of women also predate these revolutions, the momentum for social change in the late 1700s certainly served as a catalyst for greater interest in women's issues. The abolitionist movement in the early to mid 1800s in the United States furthered the feminist cause there, providing some of the rhetoric and forums for public discussions of the role of women in society. This focus on women's rights in society is often called the 'first wave' of feminist activism. But by the late 1960s – spurred by civil rights activism as well as union and student uprisings – feminist activity burgeoned in new directions and with heightened vigor. Feminists seeing these developments as a 'next generation' of activism, called it the 'second wave.' On this generational model, 'third wave' is generally understood to begin in the 1990s. Feminism is indeed one of the most important, if not *the* most important, social movement of the twentieth century. It continues to reach into new areas of study and activity, perhaps even inspiring a 'fourth wave.' Although the notion that feminism comes in generations is controversial and risks misconstruing the feminist project, looking at the waves as thematic categories provides a useful overview of feminist theory and activism.

The waves terminology is helpful insofar as it indicates a project that is not yet completed. Two main interpretations of the waves exist. The first is the chronological or generations model and the second is the thematic model. I follow the second in this book but it is worth pausing to examine the chronological model briefly.

Like waves on the ocean with ebbs and flows, the chronological or generational model of the waves of feminism purports to chart the varying intensity of feminist activity in different time periods. Accordingly, first wave feminism spans the seventeenth through the early part of the twentieth century. Some people then see an ebbing in feminist activity in the mid twentieth century. After most Western countries granted women the right to cast a vote in local and national elections, the generational model suggests there was a pause in feminist activism.

In the United States, women got the vote in 1920 and in Britain it was 1928. It took until 1944 for France to grant women full suffrage and 1971 for Switzerland. But that is far from the end of the story. Women are still denied the vote in many places in the world. Suffrage is an ongoing struggle and the right to vote is not always as secure in nations around the world as we might hope.

According to the chronological account of the waves of feminist thought the second wave begins somewhere between 1948 and 1960 and peaks from 1960 until the early 1990s. Whereas the first wave focused on women gaining status as human beings with full civil, intellectual, social, economic, and legal rights, the second wave turns to look at other sources of oppression. Many manifestations of sexist oppression are not resolved solely through the acquisition of rights or equal treatment. Women's bodies are sites of domination, stereotyping, violence, and oppression. By shifting the scope of analysis to include aspects of women's physical existence or experience, second wave feminism also sought solidarity among all women in the experience of oppression. Sisterhood, it was argued, could be a powerful political force to bring about cultural change. Later second wave feminism recognized the limitations of a common basis in experience of oppression – after all, women do not share the same social class or race.

This recognition of diversity issued forth the third wave of feminism in the mid 1990s according to the chronological account. Third wave feminism is characterized by a rejection of the project of sisterhood in favor of diversity not only in identity but in subjectivity and thought itself. Here, the site of oppression is in thought and language. The very structures of consciousness have been colonized by oppression. Third wave theories and practices employ a number of mainstream and alternative cultural techniques to challenge dominant ways of thinking and introduce new elements into personal and cultural consciousness.

Some feminists argue that we are now in a fourth wave that focuses on women's physical accomplishments and possibilities. Others call this a postfeminism in which feminist ideas of women's power are used to market products ranging from athletic wear to soap.

A variation of the chronological account of the waves describes the second wave as employing traditional political theory and applying it to women. The third wave, accordingly, offers women-centered political theory rather than modifying the traditional masculine theories. This method of interpreting the waves, however, overlooks much of the origins of feminist theory in feminist praxis. That is, that feminism in theory is a direct response to what women are doing to resist sexist oppression rather than or in addition to responses to canonical theories that exclude women.

The thematic approach is another way to think about the waves of feminism. In this approach, the metaphorical waves are concentric circles rather than generational moments. Consider, for instance, that economic and legal inequalities based on gender are often the most visible forms of oppression of women. If we think of addressing these as analogous to the first circle formed when a rain drop hits a pond, we could see that there will likely be many reverberations, some more predictable than others, and all reliant on each other. But there will also likely be countless other raindrops all over the pond. The concentric circles of all these drops blend and merge. In this thematic approach, the first wave of feminism focuses on efforts to obtain rights and formal equality. Second wave feminism expands on these accomplishments by offering a wider analysis of oppression and exploring how oppression affects identity and agency. The third wave turns to the structures of consciousness and language to see how oppression is reproduced there and how it might be fought.

Although the chronological model is significantly rooted in Western history and reveals some of the dialogues and debates among feminists, there are many reasons to favor the thematic model of the waves over the chronological. First, a chronological model misconstrues the history of feminism as singular and linear. Feminism is and ought to be understood as plural, multiple, and varied. There are many schools of thought and approaches to feminism – a single historical trajectory could not possibly account for the wide variety of thought across the globe that counts as feminist.

Second, the chronological waves appear to be class and race based; they trace the development of white, middle class feminism. But it is a mistake to disregard the anti-racism movements that helped open doors for feminism and feminists. Women of all nationalities, social classes, races, and ethnicities, have been engaged in the struggles for gender justice.

Third, the chronological model appears to assume that once one wave ends, another begins. That is, it makes it seem that the accomplishments of one wave are either presumed, taken for granted, or even opposed as obsolete by the next. This too is misleading at best and more aptly simply false. To give but one example, feminists continue to fight for legal rights and to maintain the legal rights that their predecessors obtained.

Fourth, the chronological waves privilege a particular view of feminism (this is akin to the singular history criticism). The chronological waves most closely resemble the development of feminism in the United States and Western Europe. Other feminists, other feminisms, other movements around the globe would certainly order things differently – or even point out that so many of the issues pertaining to the separate waves must be tackled simultaneously.

Finally, another criticism of thinking of feminism in terms of generations is that doing so misleadingly assumes a particular idea about progress. That assumption needs to be carefully scrutinized and challenged. In fact, as I mentioned earlier in this chapter, part of the project of feminism in general is to continually critique itself. At least part of that is a recognition that some of the causes we fight for or the arguments we make may actually be counterproductive for the overall feminist movement, exclusive of some women, or otherwise fail to account for some of the needs of some women. Nevertheless, it cannot be denied that feminism has made some striking advances in the past two centuries and that, by and large, the situation for women is improving in many parts of the world.

The thematic interpretation of the waves acknowledges different histories, issues, and causes within feminism thereby avoiding at least some of the problems of the chronological model. Issues of feminism may be clustered according to the themes in each wave. The following chapters are organized around prominent issues and debates within feminism that roughly correspond to the topics of the waves as I have presented them here. Importantly, I do not purport to offer a history of feminism and readers are encouraged not to adopt the chronological or generational model of the waves of feminism. Feminism is an ongoing plurality of projects and debates – rich in content, influence, and possibility.

The future of feminism

On the beach, when a wave hits, it makes a tremendous impact. Standing on the shore, we notice debris that gets washed away and sand, rocks, shells, and other tidal treasures washed ashore. After a while, the rhythm of the waves becomes less noticeable but that doesn't change their impact on the shore. We would certainly wonder what has happened if the waves simply stopped.

The waves of feminism are no different. When new developments in feminist theory and activism emerge, they are often met with a combination of shock and resistance. But very often, these new developments gradually work their way through society and take up residence in our mainstream ways of thinking. As waves recede or sometimes crash against each other, significant social change is left in their wake.

At the beginning of this chapter I asked 'who is a feminist?' People come to feminism in a variety of ways. Some of us are inspired by strong women leaders, some of us are led to feminism by our mothers, sisters, and friends, and others might discover feminism in a book – and, of course, many of us turn to feminism in search of solidarity in our suffering or solidarity in our resistance struggles. Somewhat paradoxically, as feminism becomes more 'mainstream' or gains traction in popular culture, the 'F-word' (feminism) becomes more threatening to some women and men. Perhaps that is simply because of the long history of political activism with which it is associated. Or perhaps some people today are reluctant to take a political stance that demands confrontation. Of course, when a person actually experiences sexism or gender violence, it becomes easier to take an oppositional stance in political solidarity with other feminists.

All too often, feminists are portrayed as militant and serious – which may also explain the reluctance on the part of some to claim the label. Although there certainly are feminists who are militant and most of us are serious at least some of the time, the stereotype is simply a way to dismiss the sound arguments for social justice that feminists make. For that reason, it might be important to mention one last feminist strategy that has been present in every form of feminism: laughter. Laughter is used as social critique of oppressive policies and actions, as political resistance to unjust treatment, and as social support for one another in the face of sometimes brutal dismissal. Laughter is a powerful tool against the serious and sometimes tragic force of sexism. As feminists, we also have to laugh at ourselves sometimes. Our failures are lessons and our proposals will sometimes be met with social ridicule. Laughing back, rather than buying into the dominant culture's assessment, might be a way to recover from the defeat and fight back with more resolve the next time. Laughter might just dispel some of those myths about feminism that close off the possibility for an open conversation about the pain, suffering, and violence of sexism.

Every few years, the popular media asks about the future of feminism or whether feminism is obsolete. And always the answer is 'feminism is far from obsolete.' Just when some feminist gains are made, others slip away. In the 1980s and 1990s, television advertisements and shows made at least some effort to avoid overt sexual objectification of women. But more recent programs and ads make fairly explicit woman's status as object. Perhaps one could argue that this is part of women's third wave reclaiming of their bodies, sexualities, and rights to be feminine but perhaps there are also adverse effects on all women. Certainly some people have argued that we are in a postfeminist era but that could mean either that feminism is obsolete and women are no longer oppressed, or that feminism has morphed into other concerns that might more aptly be termed 'humanism.' Some people even claim the name 'postfeminist' as a way to indicate women claiming the power to manipulate and control through the overt use of sexualized bodies. Not surprisingly perhaps, some feminists call such a position 'anti-feminist' rather than 'postfeminist.'

But even more than the continual ebb and flow of backlash against feminist gains, feminism will never be obsolete so long as oppression still exists. One of the developments within feminism chronicled in this book is the recognition that feminism is not just about women obtaining equality with men. Far from it. Equality with men may not even be a desirable goal if equality is built on a masculinist-limited conception of self and society.

It might be worth asking whether the expansion of feminist concerns well beyond those things that directly affect women in their social circles or geographic regions puts us in a fourth wave of feminist theory – perhaps with global and transnational feminisms leading the way. Alternatively, it might be more productive for us to think of the waves as dissipating. Rather than seeking stark divisions between approaches or themes within feminism, perhaps we should instead look for the many possibilities for productive coalitions. Feminism has already expanded its self-understanding in such a way that all systems of domination are targets for feminist theory and action. By applying the same rule to ourselves as feminists, we stand a better chance of avoiding domination, competition, and division within feminism.

Feminists do not always or even regularly agree. Different ideological goals and different methodologies sometimes cause quite violent rifts between feminists – seas are rarely serenely calm after all. But in spite of disagreements, there is a lot more in common among feminists. Feminists look at the world differently. We understand that subtle things such as language can have a big impact on how a person experiences the world. This critical awareness compels us to action – whether through writing, speaking, confronting, protesting, or otherwise refusing to do the expected. Moreover, feminists and all social activists will have to continue to look for new forms of praxis suitable to the ever-changing world.

Political coalitions are not always consciously chosen or explicitly linked. So it has been with feminism. In fact, it would be more accurate to refer to 'feminisms' in the plural. It is a movement, an academic discipline, a way of life, a political commitment, a cultural relation, and so much more.

It is impossible to tell what feminism will look like in the next ten, twenty, fifty years. I think most feminists would like to see a mass based movement that incorporates care for the earth as well as new social and political structures that ensure the ability to contribute and values the contributions of all people regardless of gender, sexual orientation, ability, class, age, geographical location, colonial past, and any other category that has been used to marginalize and exclude. Alas, new forms of oppression and violence emerge all the time – and we humans are amazingly tenacious with our grip on old prejudices. I used to say, only half jokingly, that if I did my job well, I would eventually put myself out of work. (If we use the waves metaphor, I suppose that would mean that I was all washed up!) As a feminist writer, teacher, and activist, doing my job well would mean playing a part in the creation of a world free from oppression and domination, especially sex and gender based oppression and domination. Feminism certainly still has an important role to play in the world.

2

Schools of feminist thought

Feminists are usually motivated by something in deciding to act to resist sexist oppression. Often that motivation is some sort of personal harm or the realization that women as a group are harmed. We can loosely group different motivations into schools of thought. These help to illustrate what goals feminists might have as well as providing some justification for pursuing some actions rather than others.

While it is not always easy or desirable to put any given feminist into a particular school of thought, understanding the different schools helps to uncover agendas for social change and reveals some ideological disagreements among feminists. I will discuss eight different schools of feminist theory, most from the Anglo-American tradition, and compare their accounts of the oppression of women as well as their strategies for liberation. It should be kept in mind, however, that while these categories reveal the richly divergent types of feminism, they are not necessarily mutually exclusive, exclusionary, or comprehensive. There are many ways to understand the oppression of women and numerous varieties of feminism.

Liberal feminism

The first two schools of feminist theory get at least some of their inspiration from classical political theory. They are *Liberal feminism* and *Marxist feminism*. As the name indicates, liberal feminism draws on classical liberalism for a specifically feminist theory. In doing so, liberal feminism adopts the liberal conceptions of human nature and human freedom and uses these to articulate a vision for feminist liberation. Liberalism holds that humans are rational, autonomous individuals. Part of acting rationally is acting so as to maximize one's self-interest and often this takes the form of competition. With its roots in social contract theory, especially the classical versions of Hobbes and Locke, liberalism focuses on freedom or liberty for the individual. Rousseau's social contract theory adds an emphasis on equality but his conception of equality is so far reaching that he is not always classed among the classical liberals. Broadly speaking, liberalism holds that each of us ought to be free to pursue our own version of the good life.

Feminists who build on this foundation of classical liberalism identify the roots of the oppression of women in the lack of legal rights and equal opportunities accorded to women. By looking at how the state views women and addressing those areas where women are disadvantaged, liberal feminists believe that the oppression of women might be ameliorated. For instance, consider that in many Western societies it is only recently that women were considered full citizens rather than merely members of families represented by the male head of household, or that women were not allowed to own property or sign contracts, or were protected from rape not as persons but as the property of their husbands or fathers. Of course, obtaining equal opportunities for women and awarding equal legal rights is much more complex than it might appear at first glance.

Feminists first have to argue that women are fully human, and in the context of liberalism, that means arguing that women have the same capacity for rationality that men have. Not just the social and legal practices but also metaphysical and epistemological assumptions that support them must be scrutinized. In keeping with classical liberalism, most liberal feminists adopt the traditional epistemological position that knowledge is objectively verifiable and value neutral. If, for example, we could all adopt the point of view of the impartial observer, then we should all come up with the true knowledge about the world. However, if women are not admitted to the realm of 'knowers' in the same manner as men, then women's education will be structured differently than men's, a point I discuss further in Chapter 3 in 'Social, legal, and economic rights for women.'

Among the many campaigns of liberal feminists are the struggle to allow women into the universities and workplaces on a par with men; the struggle for equal pay for equal work; the struggle to gain admission to social roles, clubs, and events reserved solely for men, and similar efforts to obtain equal liberty to pursue each woman's own vision of the good life.

Marxist feminism

In contrast to the liberal feminist arguments about women's oppression and possibilities for liberation, the Marxist feminist holds that it is the material conditions of life, rather than legal barriers, that inhibit women's freedom. Whereas liberal feminists identify legal, social, and intellectual inequality as the roots of the oppression of women, Marxist feminists claim that capitalism causes women's oppressed situation in society. As their name indicates, Marxist feminists rely on and build on Marxist theory; class oppression, for Marxists, is the foundation of all other forms of oppression and the most pervasive as well. The first and arguably most important Marxist feminist was Karl Marx's long time intellectual partner Friedrich Engels.

In *The Origin of the Family, Private Property, and the State*, Friedrich Engels uses Marx's critique of capitalism and the method of historical materialism (a method that analyzes human history from the perspective of materialism, the understanding

'The overthrow of mother-right was the world historical defeat of the female sex. The man took command in the home also; the woman was degraded and reduced to servitude, she became the slave of his lust and a mere instrument for the production of children.'

Friedrich Engels, *The Origin of the Family, Private Property, and the State* (1884).

that it is the material aspects of human existence that are *real*) to trace the emergence of the oppression of women. By looking at how production changes through history, Engels argues, we can see how women's power in the family changed. Whereas families were originally matrilineal (since, after all, women are the only ones who know for sure who their children are), a change in production – that is a change in the way humans meet their material needs – brought about a change in the familial structure as well. Engels marks the domestication of animals, origin of private property, and the overthrow of the 'mother-right' as the 'world historical defeat of the female sex.' Men became the 'owners' of the means of production and women's social status decreased significantly. Moreover, Engels shows how laws regulating adultery were instituted to protect the private property of the male head of house.

Subsequent Marxist feminists have continued Engels' line of argument by looking at women's role within capitalism today. One of the most important contemporary Marxist feminist arguments is over wages for housework. Capitalism relies on a class of people doing 'reproductive' labor that is unremunerated (including everything from bearing and raising children to making lunches, mending socks, and caring for the elderly). Marxist feminists have variously argued that this work done in the reproductive sphere be valued as productive and paid or be socialized so that women are not relegated to this unpaid workforce.

Marxist feminism is unique among schools of feminist thought insofar as it posits an historical starting point for the oppression of women. If the roots of oppression are found in class society and private property under capitalism, then theoretically, in order to get rid of the oppression of women, capitalism itself must be abolished. This begins with the abolition of a class society and private property. Women must be part of the productive sphere or part of public industry. Moreover, as Engels argued, the family as an economic unit must be abolished. This latter suggestion implies that every adult would work for a wage and that marriages would not be based on economic necessity. It would not necessarily mean that there would be no marriages or families.

Although this summary of Marxist feminism is brief, it shows the centrality of the economic structure of society in understanding and alleviating the oppression of women. Freedom, according to Marxist feminists and Marxists, is understood not as some purified notion of autonomy but as the absence of the coercion of economic necessity. Similarly, the social and political value of equality is defined not as formal civil equality but as the absence of social class divisions and approximate equality in the ability to satisfy material needs.

Radical feminism

Marxist feminists blame capitalism for the oppression of women but there is another ideological system that many feminists believe is even more fundamental and pernicious: patriarchy. Generally speaking, patriarchy denotes a social organization that systematically oppresses women and benefits men. The origin of the word, meaning rule by the father, is in political theory but radical feminists mean more than the political organization of society when they use the word.

Patriarchy means a whole network or system of control of women and women's bodies by men. It is a power structure that identifies women on the basis of their biological sex and, in particular, their reproductive abilities. Radical feminists see the root of female oppression as sex based childbearing and childrearing roles and the identification of women with their sexualized bodies. Another way to think about this is simply to ask 'What makes men and women different?' More often than not the average person would offer a biologically based answer. It is that answer then that radical feminists hold up as the source of the oppression of women. Because women can bear children they have been relegated to the private sphere of the family or domestic life, they are held responsible for reproduction (and men are excused from reproductive activities), and sexual intercourse is defined by the pleasure of men. Monogamous heterosexuality, accordingly, is an enforced norm rather than a free choice. It is used as an ideological tool to keep women subservient to men socially and ensure men's power over women's sexuality.

Radical feminists suggest a number of possible solutions to this oppression and most are, well, quite radical. They are meant to be. By proposing rather extreme solutions to the problem of the oppression of women, radical feminists provoke us to think more imaginatively about our social interactions and gender roles. For instance, one solution is to use our technological advances to replace biological reproduction with technological reproduction. Infants could be gestated externally in incubators or pods. This would free women from the 'tyranny of reproductive biology' while also opening more avenues for men to participate in the reproductive process. If oppression is based on an unjust power relation and abolishing oppression means abolishing such relations, and if women have a power that men do not have – even if it is currently used against them – then, some radical feminists argue, women ought to give up that power as well. This proposal is not as fanciful as it may seem. The technological advances in reproductive health appear to make extra-utero gestation a real possibility. Of course, one criticism of this proposal as a radical feminist proposal is that if the technology remains in the hands of men, then women's social position remains unchanged or even becomes more oppressive. Another criticism is that such a technological revolution would take away the one power that women have. This latter point is made by cultural feminists and the reasoning behind it is discussed below.

In defense of the radical feminist proposal, abolishing biological reproduction would go a long way in abolishing the sex and gender roles in society. Freedom would be an expansive concept that included freedom from those roles. Families could be reconceived in new and fluid ways. Rather than the traditional, heterosexual family, families might be homosexual, single parent, group (much like a community or shared parenting extended family arrangement), or any number of other varieties of arrangements. To a radical feminist, women cannot be free until they are free to make their own decisions about their bodies, and especially, their reproductive abilities.

It is probably evident that by positing patriarchy as the central ideology that oppresses women, the radical feminist position understands human nature as primarily structured by a sex-gender system. Human beings are embodied sexual beings and their reproductive capacities determine their place in society. Regardless of whether women's childrearing abilities are 'natural' or not, the radical feminist sees women as defined and determined – hence oppressed – by those abilities or by that embodied sexual role. But the sex-determined social roles are not the full extent of the oppression of women. Everything from language and knowledge to economics and literature, according to some radical feminists, is affected by enforced heterosexuality and the biologically based roles in reproduction. Such an entrenched system of oppression requires pretty radical solutions for overcoming it.

Shulamith Firestone's book, *The Dialectic of Sex* (1970), utilizes the logic of Marx's dialectical materialism but replaces class division with sex. Firestone argues that the sex dichotomy is the most fundamental division in society and that all forms of oppression (racial, class, age, etc.) are modeled on the oppression of women by men. Biological reproduction, according to Firestone, is the root of women's oppression because the sex based childbearing roles ground and are used to justify sex based childrearing roles as well as other divisions within society. Her proposals to abolish this oppression are among the most far reaching and visionary (some might say outlandish) in feminist theory. In addition to what she describes as 'the freeing of women from the tyranny of their reproductive biology,' Firestone calls for a sharing of childrearing and *bearing* roles. Clearly this would call for something like the technological revolution described above. But Firestone also argues that children are oppressed too and, importantly, that their oppression is intertwined with the oppression of women. Women need children in order to have a place in the patriarchal system but children also learn the rules and roles of patriarchy from women. For this reason, Firestone advocates social, economic, and sexual liberation of children as well as women. Children should be free to explore their sexuality unencumbered by the dictates of society.

> Firestone famously described childbirth in *The Dialectic of Sex* as 'like shitting a pumpkin.'

Taking sex as fundamental or foundational to the oppressive structure of society also means scrutinizing how women's bodies are used, portrayed, or otherwise represented. Andrea Dworkin and Catharine MacKinnon are two prominent radical feminists who gained widespread public attention for their anti-pornography efforts. They argued that pornography was symptomatic of male control of female sexuality in society. Dworkin and Mackinnon pushed to make pornography illegal in Minneapolis and Indianapolis and also influenced pornography rulings elsewhere. They defined pornography as 'the graphic sexually explicit subordination of women, whether in pictures or in words' and further elucidate this definition by stating that sexual subordination might include the sexual objectification of women as conquered, dominated, or servile; as enjoying pain, humiliation, rape, mutilation, or physical abuse; or otherwise violated by objects or animals. They further specify that pornography in this definition extends to anyone subject to the degradation described (males, children, transsexuals). The role of 'woman' in the definition is an indication of the person dominated. Pornography, they argue, makes violence against women – both extreme forms of violence and more mundane forms of degradation – appear common place or acceptable. In other words, pornography is not just direct violence to women; it is also a sort of training ground for the mental, physical, and emotional violence men do to women every day.

Although many people find radical feminism a bit too far reaching in its social critique, and some people even say radical feminism is passé, many feminists continue to offer provocative radical proposals that do help identify problems of women's oppression and offer innovative solutions for social change.

Socialist feminism

Another school of feminist theory tries to blend the critique of patriarchy with the critique of capitalism. Socialist feminists argue that both ideological systems adversely affect women and that both need to be fought. As the name indicates, they take some direction from socialist thinkers (especially the utopian socialists) but the socialist movements of the nineteenth and twentieth centuries were often quite sexist in their policies and practices. Socialist feminists hope to infuse some feminist politics into the socialist agenda while avoiding some of the extremes of both the Marxist feminists and the radical feminists. The next question is how, and there are multiple models among socialist feminists for addressing both patriarchy and capitalism.

One of the key differences between radical, Marxist, and socialist feminism is just how they understand the cause or roots of the oppression of women. Radical feminists say the oppression is due to women's biological role in reproduction or women's place in a sex divided society; Marxist feminists say it is capitalism; and socialist feminists say both are true and then try to discern how capitalism and patriarchy are connected. Of course the connection might be deep down and some socialist feminists opt to seek the 'unifying concept': some underlying thing that not only links capitalism and patriarchy but perhaps explains all forms of oppression. If we imagine that each form of oppression is a branch of a very large tree, then when we recognize the 'unifying concept' we thereby can understand better the conceptual structure of oppression, and we can tear out all oppression by its roots rather than continuing to trim away at branches that seemingly continue to grow and even flourish in spite of near constant attack. A number of contenders for the unifying concept have been discussed in feminist literature. One is the 'division of labor.' This makes sense because both patriarchy and capitalism employ some sort of division of labor whether it is based on sex or class. Though, of course, there are limits to the gender division of labor. Other possibilities for a unifying concept are 'systems of domination,' 'alienation,' and 'either/or dichotomous thinking.' Each of these is evident in all forms of oppression, albeit in different ways. But, as with the gender division of labor, there might also be problems with each of these. As a critical project, feminism has to not only make proposals but also scrutinize those proposals for their strengths and weaknesses.

Some socialist feminists argue that capitalism and patriarchy are indistinguishable. Heidi Hartmann, for instance, famously argues that patriarchy is a material condition or economic relation that serves the collective effort of men dominating women. She claims that the sexual division of labor, which mandates that women care for children and men work in the public sphere, maintains women's subordination in all aspects of society. Accordingly, fighting patriarchy will be unsuccessful unless capitalism is also overthrown.

Other socialist feminists consider capitalism and patriarchy two different ideological systems that run parallel to each other. Each oppresses women in different ways and each requires different approaches for overcoming that oppression. For instance, one might analyze sexism much like the radical feminist noting the biological roots of women's role in the family and exclusion from public and political activities. That same feminist might see capitalism as accounting for some of the economic exploitation of the work that women do in the home. In other words, women's reproductive capacity as well as capitalism's reliance on a large unpaid work force combine to create the oppression of women.

The solutions proposed by socialist feminists vary but they are united in their effort to transform or end capitalism and patriarchy. At times, the proposals to end oppression are more revolutionary than others but socialist feminists generally agree that challenging patriarchy without challenging the class divisions in society, or challenging class division without addressing sex based divisions will not adequately alleviate the oppression of women. They also tend to agree that it is counter-productive for feminists to argue over which form of oppression is worse or which form ought to take precedence. Instead, as the unifying concept shows, socialist feminism argues that all forms of oppression are interrelated or interconnected.

Women's liberation, indeed all liberation, for the socialist feminist is understood as freedom from the social and historical class and gender roles. But even beyond that, socialist feminists emphasize the self-determination of each individual within a community. There is a balance between the individual and the community. Both are important and individual rights should not trump communal obligations. One assumption here is that individuals already are in community. Human beings are biological creatures whose identities or natures are influenced by the community within which they live as well as their physical being and environmental context. Metaphysical and epistemological claims about women must take this conglomeration of influences into account. Some feminists associate socialist feminism with 'standpoint epistemology' which is discussed in Chapter 4. Suffice it to say that standpoint epistemology is a theory of knowledge that holds that knowledge claims are affected by (or even determined by) the standpoint or social position one occupies. This is quite different from liberal feminism which maintains that objectivity in science and knowledge is possible.

Cultural feminism

Another school of feminist thought is 'cultural feminism.' I mentioned it earlier when discussing the unique power of women in the reproductive process. In a way, this name is quite misleading but if we can think of women's contributions to social existence as a sort of 'culture' then perhaps the name is appropriate. Whereas radical feminists focus on biological sex as the root of oppression, cultural feminists focus on gender. That is, the root of women's oppression is that the specifically feminine attributes within any given society are devalued.

In most Western societies, caring or nurturing capacities are unappreciated, unacknowledged, or excluded from politics and morality generally. This devaluation of caring oppresses women because women are traditionally the primary providers of care within families and society. To devalue care is to devalue the women who do the caring. As one might guess, women are in something of a double-bind. The caring work that they do is not adequately acknowledged or appreciated and yet society relies on it and often faults women who fail to fulfill it. Moreover, there is an extension of this critique to epistemology as well. Women's ways of knowing – often identified as intuitive or maternal – are excluded from those categories of knowledge claims that are considered valid sources.

Perhaps the most important contribution to cultural feminism was Carol Gilligan's study of the moral psychological patterns of boys and girls published in the classic book *In a Different Voice* (1982). Gilligan's research suggested that women tend to respond to moral dilemmas by focusing on the relationships of the participants in the scenario. Men, on the other hand, tend to focus on individual rights. This tendency is a difference (a 'different voice') that contributes a new model for moral decision making based on the experience of women.

Strong versions of cultural feminism argue for essential feminine traits that are more peaceful, nurturing, intuitive, and life affirming. Weaker versions eschew the essentialist claim but nonetheless posit some set of characteristics that women have that makes them fundamentally different from men. According to other schools of feminist thought, those characteristics could, of course, find their origins in a patriarchal system that requires women to be nurturing of children and men but, according to the cultural feminist, the central point is that women have these traits. Oppression is understood as a failure to appreciate care and nurturing as central to human existence. Women's activities as caregivers in the family help to infuse some of those life affirming values in society but cultural feminists would be quick to add that a lot more needs to be done both to value the work that women do in the family and to facilitate more compassion throughout every sphere of social existence.

One influential theoretical example of the attempts to transform social existence by permeating it with care is Sara Ruddick's book *Maternal Thinking* (1995). Maternal thinking is the specific type of thinking a mother uses (and Ruddick is careful to say that 'mothers' are people who fulfill a particular role in childrearing – they need not be female but often are). In particular, she argues that women engage in the practices of protection, nurturance, and training. These practices arise out of the needs of children. Children demand 'preservation' which means that they must be protected. Much of the work that mothers do is a sort of protection; mothers protect against such things as hunger, harm, and neglect. Further, children need assistance in their growth processes. Mothers provide the age appropriate nurturance to aid this development. And finally, the training mothers provide is training in what Ruddick calls 'social acceptability.' Ruddick was inspired in part by her own mothering experience and the rich wisdom she found in talking with other mothers at playgrounds, schools, and other child-centered activities. That wisdom was not acknowledged as wisdom at all by mainstream theories of knowledge and rarely given much respect or credence by popular culture either. Ruddick demonstrates how knowledge emerges from the practices of mothers. The practices are constantly changing; mothers and maternal thinking must change to meet new challenges.

Ruddick further argues that maternal thinking can and should be the basis for a specifically feminist peace politics. She draws on her own experience in social movements as well as the narratives of other mother-activists to demonstrate the usefulness of maternal thinking for politics. The motivation and methods of these mother-activists brought a different focus to peace politics: one grounded in care. In other words, Ruddick argued that maternal practices and maternal thinking could be and probably should be suffused throughout society rather than confined to familial relations. As one can see, maternal thinking is more pacifist than other forms of thinking and Ruddick and other cultural feminists rely on that notion in suggesting wider social change based on care.

Care and nurturing generally are not considered widely accepted social values in liberal societies. Indeed, many of the obstacles to women's participation in public and political life revolve around an assumption that women's compassion would get in the way of acting rationally. For the cultural feminist, however, rationality and compassion or care are not mutually exclusive or otherwise opposed to each other. Liberation can only be realized if men and women are free to care within any social context. The logic of non-violence, as is evident from Ruddick's peace politics, replaces the logic of war and even the logic of competition. Imagine, for instance, a business model that sought to facilitate or nurture the full potential of everyone concerned in a transaction. Such a model would contrast rather sharply with the competitive model that seeks to maximize self-interest.

One of the great debates of the last two decades in moral theory is between justice and care. If care is feminine, some people argued, then justice is masculine. The relation between the two formed the subject of the debate. I say a bit more about this in Chapter 4 but it is worth mentioning here that the vast majority of cultural feminists do not seek to unseat justice as a normative moral value but to highlight the importance of care and compassion with or within justice.

Womanist theory

Of course, the very idea that we can identify *the* source of women's oppression – as if it is a single source or single cause and is experienced by all women in exactly the same manner – is not only misleading, it is also quite alienating for many women. Some women who struggle against sexist oppression are quite put off by feminist arguments no matter whether they are liberal, radical, socialist, or some combination of these. Womanist theory is a sort of challenge to traditional articulations of feminist theory. By explicitly rejecting the name 'feminist,' proponents force a re-examination of what counts as 'feminist.' In particular, Womanist theory looks at the intersections between race, class, and gender. Individual women's lives are, after all, not just affected by their sex or gender status. Women face countless other social forces that stereotype, violate, objectify, and dominate.

Womanist thought has some roots in Black Liberation Theology. Like the other schools of feminist thought, there really is no unified body of theory. Instead, the name connotes a category that broadly identifies some concerns and issues. One prominent African American feminist theorist, bell hooks (who puts her chosen pseudonym, based on matrilineal relations, in lower case as an explicit rejection of patriarchal naming and control of women) suggests, many women reject the term 'feminism' precisely because there are so many varieties of feminisms. Such bifurcation appears to indicate that there is no solidarity among women. It might also suggest that feminism is more concerned with ideological debates within the academy than it is with effecting social change for real women everywhere. Another reason, according to hooks, is that feminism itself has often been a racist movement – an effort to make white middle and upper class women equivalent to white middle and upper class men. By ignoring the way race and class affect black women, feminism, according to hooks, fails in its project. Moreover, many of the issues that a white, middle class feminist would understand as central are either contradicted by the experience of many black women or are peripheral to their experience.

Instead, hooks argues for a redefinition of feminism as 'a struggle to end sexist oppression.' There are a number of salient points about this definition. As a struggle, feminism is necessarily a revolutionary collective movement. She makes a distinction between feminism as a lifestyle choice and a political movement. As a lifestyle choice, individual feminists make only a commitment to themselves and enact a feminist agenda only through the personal decisions they make. There is no necessary connection to others or to creating social change. Feminism in that sense might merely be reforming some particular social practices that adversely affect an individual woman. In contrast, as a political movement, feminism is a wider commitment to others, to actively work to bring about positive change in the lives of women affected by sexist oppression. It is political and it is collective. By 'sexist oppression' hooks means all those forms of oppression that affect women's political existence. Racism, classism, ableism, heterosexism, ageism, and multiple other forms of oppression are experienced by women daily but, of course, all women do not experience all of these. The key is that there is a cultural basis for oppression. In efforts solely focused on the eradication of one form of oppression, the underlying roots of all forms remain in place. This is similar in many respects to the socialist feminist project of identifying a unifying concept. For hooks, 'the cultural basis of group oppression' is rooted at least in part in either/or thinking. Either/or thinking is found in all forms of domination in Western society, according to hooks. We categorize people into two mutually exclusive groups but these two groups do not exist in equilibrium. Domination makes one group subordinate and one group superior (think, for instance, of the dichotomies Men/Women, White/Black, Rich/Poor).

In addition to hooks' proposals, Womanist solutions include intersectionality or intersectional thinking. Intersectionality was first suggested by legal scholar Kimberlé Crenshaw who noticed the way race was left out of most feminist domestic violence and rape discourses and how the gendered nature of these crimes were often obscured by some of the dominant discourses in the black community. Intersectional thinking aims to avoid privileging any particular voice – neither one's race nor one's sex are primary. Instead, human beings are, in a sense, products of their sex, race, and class experiences. All knowledge is affected by these experiences and cultural codes (some of which are oppressive and some of which are dominating). Crenshaw argued that intersectional thinking was not only desirable but necessary to adequately and accurately challenge the violence in women's lives, especially black women's lives.

All of the different schools of feminist thought have a particular way of characterizing freedom or liberation. In the case of Womanist thought, the emphasis is on the full self-development of everyone but there is also a recognition that we are all involved with families, communities, political entities, and other groups that affect our self-development in important ways. The key (and there is a sense that this applies to all of the schools) is that no one ought to be subject to domination of any sort. In order to bring out this vision, however, more attention needs to be paid to the ways in which forms of oppression intersect, interconnect, or overlap.

Postmodern feminism

The next school of feminist thought is a bit more difficult to describe precisely because of the very nature of postmodernism. Postmodernism rejects 'grand narratives,' or more or less comprehensive explanatory theories. So, in discussing postmodern feminism we should not think of it as a theory but rather as a collection of ideas. Of course, all of the schools of thought thus far discussed might similarly be described as collections of similar ideas. What makes postmodern feminism different is the refusal to look for a single explanation for the oppression of women. Three ideas that figure prominently in postmodern feminist thought are phallologocentrism, psychoanalysis, and sexual difference.

Phallocentrism (somewhat distinct from phallologocentrism) literally means the centrality of the phallus. The phallus is the symbolic representation of the penis. Phallologocentrism, or sometimes phallogocentrism, adds the 'centrality of the word.' *Logos*, the root of logic and all those 'ologies' we study, means a variety of different things given the context. It means word, law, principle, thought, etc. Postmodern feminism looks to the structure of consciousness to see that thought and language are masculine-centered, hence phallologocentrism. The centrality of the phallus, however, means something slightly different than what radical feminists might describe as 'male oriented' or liberal feminists might call 'a man's world.' Instead, postmodern feminists argue that the singularity of the penis as the male sex organ symbolically represents the singularity of thought. Think, for instance, of how language is learned. Small children see the world in a wide array of colors but are taught to call fairly divergent colors 'red.' In that process, they are taught to think of the world according to certain categories. There is, in effect, a singular right way of looking at the colors of the world.

In contrast, a postmodern feminist emphasizes diversity and difference. They see otherness not as a detriment but as something to be celebrated. Hélène Cixous, as a novelist, challenged women to engage in feminine writing (*l'écriture feminine*) and contrast it with masculine writing (*literatur*). Masculine writing bears the marks of phallocentrism (and Cixous famously drew the analogy of Penis/phallus/pen). *L'écriture feminine* was an attempt to write in a way that challenges the rules governing language and grammar. Women were to write the unthought/unthinkable so as to dare to confront women's place in the world. Writing women's bodies calls for 'white ink' instead of black and here Cixous is drawing a literary reference to breast milk. Through its openness and overt challenge to the structures and content of writing, feminine writing helps practice subversive thought. Whereas masculine writing is singular, feminine writing, like women's sexual experience, is multiple, varied, and pleasure-filled according to Cixous.

The second prominent concept or method for postmodern feminism is psychoanalysis. All of the major feminists who are called 'postmodern' (Hélène Cixious, Julia Kristeva, Annie LeClerc, Luce Irigaray, Judith Butler among others) make use of a method of psychoanalysis from Sigmund Freud or Jacques Lacan. Psychoanalysis gets us to look back into our childhood – or even our infantile state – to find therein the roots of our current way of thinking. Freud and Lacan were notoriously sexist in their psychoanalytic writings and the major postmodern feminists both appropriate and criticize some of the methods of psychoanalysis.

The third prominent concept is sexual difference. Here, as with phallocentrism and psychoanalysis, the postmodern feminists hold that sexual difference is socially constructed not biologically based. Language posits two genders (masculine and feminine) and while gender has been long considered a result of social conditions, the postmodernists take it a step further to say that sex too is socially and linguistically determined rather than any sort of natural fact. This helps to emphasize their allegiance to multiplicity, difference, and plurality and also challenges the very notion of 'woman.' Perhaps 'woman' itself is a fiction contrived by an oppressive linguistic structure. If the term 'woman' does not refer to any essentially defined group, then, postmodern feminists argue, the way is opened for more diversity and freedom from the oppressive dichotomous thought that characterizes so much of Western ideology.

Postmodern feminism certainly challenges readers to think in different ways but it has also been criticized for being a bit too focused on debates within the academy and not really pertinent and accessible to the vast majority of people. A related criticism is that some of the positions of postmodern feminism seem to undercut any possibility of political action on behalf of women or political unity of women.

Third World and postcolonial feminism

Third World feminism, as the name suggests, emerges from Third World women. 'Third World' here, however, should be considered a political category more than a geopolitical category. Chandra Mohanty has forcefully argued that the category 'Third World Woman' represents the coalition building and solidarity between women who make certain political commitments. These communities of women voluntarily elect to fight together to bring about social, cultural, or political change. The imperialism, racism, and sexism that constitute the existence of so many women impels some to unite in opposition and resistance. That oppositional struggle is the context for women to call themselves 'Third World Women' or 'Third World Feminists.' 'Postcolonial' is a related concept: men and women in former colonies responding to and challenging the legacy of colonialism in their past. Third World feminism and postcolonial feminism argue that the roots of oppression are in these histories of colonialism, exploitation, imperialism, sexism, and racism.

Sexism and racism take on global dimensions when we analyze the global distribution of resources. Wealthy countries take valuable assets from less developed regions of the globe and often couple this misappropriation with the dumping of waste and hazardous material. The poor of the world are multiply burdened by this exploitation and women make up the majority of the poor in the world.

Importantly, embedded in the Third World feminist analysis of oppression is also a critique of many dominant Western schools of feminist theory. While feminists from wealthy Western nations had the privilege of fighting for the right to work and participate in political life, or equal pay for equal work, women all over the developing world were fighting against often violent social and political repression. In some cases, of course, this was a struggle for survival as well. Women carry a disproportionate weight of the burden of being poor. Another way of thinking about this is to say that Third World feminist theory emphasizes the importance of histories of colonialism and how states demarcate or constrain the daily lives of their citizens. Survival itself becomes a matter of politics, not just provisions.

In thinking about liberation, Third World and postcolonial theorists emphasize history, memory, and narrative. Memory of colonial oppression helps to maintain a standpoint of resistance in liberation efforts. History is checked with racism, imperialism, sexism, and other forms of oppression that form the background for political marginalization and economic exploitation. By recognizing that human beings engaged in praxis emerge from these histories and contexts of struggle, we are better equipped to recognize the multiplicity of oppressive forces in day to day survival. There are strong alliances here with socialist feminism and Womanist theory which, like Third World feminism, aim to acknowledge the intersections and interconnections between different forms of oppression. The differences, of course, include the fact that Third World feminism tends to focus on the context of struggle or resistance rather than the similarities between types of oppression.

Another aspect of the postcolonial perspective on history draws on a Marxian critique of history. If history is recorded by the colonizers, then it will, of course, not only reflect their view of reality but also privilege their social position in the process.

Liberation is then understood as freedom from hegemonic culture and the freedom of all people (and especially women) to shape their futures according to their own visions and in light of their oppressed histories. This would also require political, economic, and social self-determination as well as freedom from sexual violence.

* * *

There are additional schools of feminist thought of course and two, ecofeminism and queer theory, will receive special attention in Chapter 5, while global feminism is discussed in Chapter 6. Regardless of what motivates feminist activism or accounts for the disagreements among feminists, all feminists agree that there is something about culture or society that harms women and that needs changing. In other words, they are united by a critical activist project that hopes to abolish sexism and related forms of oppression.

Although I have presented these schools of feminist thought as distinct, I hope it is also clear that there is significant overlap between them. In fact, it is often both futile and impossible to categorize any given feminist into any one school of thought. One feminist might embrace Marxist methods and motives for one issue and cultural feminism for another. Another feminist might be a socialist feminist most of her life and adopt ecofeminism or postcolonial feminism as her attention turns to more global issues. Nevertheless, these different approaches to feminism help us to see some of the wide diversity among feminists, their motivations, and their proposals to bring about change.

3
Social, legal, and economic rights for women: the first wave

All of the schools of feminist thought discussed in the previous chapter and so many others that I have not yet mentioned or that are still developing begin with a common assumption: women are oppressed. They differ quite dramatically in how they understand or explain that oppression, what strategies they propose for reform or revolution to overcome that oppression, and even who counts as 'woman' or whether there is such a category at all. In this chapter I look at certain forms of oppression: social, legal, political, and intellectual inequalities. These forms of oppression characterize the focus of feminism's first wave.

The first wave focuses on gaining human status; civic, social, economic, and intellectual/educational equality; and the political and legal status of women. It allows us to study a number of issues that continue to be pertinent to the lives of women and men today while also exploring some of the historical development of feminism in the Western world. This chapter is particularly focused on Anglo-American feminism because of the cultural value of rights found therein.

What does it mean to be human?

This question includes everything from whether a culture or a society considers women to be fully human to whether women are considered rational. Although these questions might strike one as absurd, it really is not so long ago in our collective history that women were not considered to be fully human or rational, and in many places around the globe women are still considered inferior sorts of beings compared to men. There is plenty of evidence that even when a culture claims to embrace equality, women are still being treated as less than fully human.

Once we establish that women are indeed human and that they are and ought to be considered full moral persons (with all the rights that accompany that status), then we can scrutinize the educational opportunities afforded to women. The right to equal education has long been a feminist concern. Some early feminists argued that we should educate girls as we educate boys rather than in the 'finishing schools' that taught girls only those skills that they might need as a bourgeois housewife. Further, the institutions of higher learning have only recently opened their doors to women. More contemporary feminist accounts of equal intellectual and educational rights discuss such things as conduct in the classroom, content of course material, and prevalence of positive role models.

We might begin with the most fundamental of questions: who counts as human? Even today in various places around the world or at various times in our own societies, women are fighting to be recognized as fully human. In the Western philosophical tradition, there are quite explicit claims to the contrary.

Aristotle (384–322 BCE), whose philosophy permeates so much of Western ideology, famously said the 'female is a deformed male.' Although his point was much more intricate and nuanced (and ought not to be separated from his metaphysical account of reproduction), this short phrase continues to carry undue weight in many contexts. Thomas Aquinas (1225–1274 CE) was heavily influenced by Aristotle and explains this line to mean that females are not misbegotten in their universal human nature but are misbegotten in their individual nature. One way to interpret this is to say that women are necessary to the species but as individual representations of the species they are incomplete at best. Aristotle and Aquinas held that the male is the more perfect of the two because he gives semen in the process of reproduction. Semen was thought to be the catalyst and perhaps even the location of the soul; the ovum was not discovered until the later part of the nineteenth century. Writing over seven hundred years earlier, Aquinas could not have known the extent of the female contribution in conception (though he certainly knew of the female's contribution to gestation).

Moral and political philosophers throughout the tradition failed to include women in their conceptions of society. This was in spite of the stage set by Plato (428/27–347 BCE) in the *Republic*. There, Plato argued that women should train alongside men and that all people ought to find their place in society based on their individual natures rather than some presumptions about the nature of the sexes. But in a later work, Plato makes an altogether different claim. In the *Timaeus*, he says that women are created from the souls of the most wicked and irrational men. Unhappily, this later sentiment had more staying power in political theory than the gender egalitarianism of the *Republic*.

Augustine of Hippo (354–430 CE) based his thought on that of Plato and sought to blend Platonic thought with Christian faith. Augustine has somewhat complicated views on women. On the one hand, he defends the full humanity of women arguing that the image of God (which is what distinguishes humans from other animals) is found in both men and women equally. The image of God is only in that part of the mind that is dedicated to the contemplation of God and both men and women share in the ability to contemplate God. But women and men also have temporal or earthly duties that are, at least in part, dictated to them by their God-given natures. Women appear to have more of these temporal duties (think, for instance, of the childbearing and nursing roles) and thus cannot devote as much of their time or intellect to the contemplation of God. So women both are and are not equal.

In their own ways, each of these addresses the question of whether women are human. It is a little too simple to say 'yes' or 'no' but clearly some early philosophers were not convinced that women are human in the same way that men are human. The more modern figure Jean-Jacques Rousseau (1712–1778) certainly thought women were human, but that they had a distinct set of natural virtues that meant they should be educated and treated differently than men. This raises a similar question regarding not the humanity of females but their moral personhood.

Rousseau's discussion of woman's moral activity focuses on her obligation to be a good wife and mother. He describes a separate set of virtues for the woman. Women were to be docile and sweet rather than courageous and wise. Rousseau assumes that a woman has no duties outside the family, and he ignores the experience of women who have no choice but to work outside the home. In other words, Rousseau's moral woman is a middle to upper class woman who has the leisure to devote all of her attentions to her husband and children. But Rousseau is not alone among traditional moral and political theorists.

Classical liberalism more generally relies on the concept of the individual as party to a social contract. But the individuals of classical liberalism are assumed to be free of household duties. Additionally, the rights of the individual that governments are meant to protect are almost always exclusively or primarily the rights of a male property owner. Women are assumed to be part of the 'person' of the man who represents the family in all public or political matters. Socialist traditions are slightly better in that women of the working class were certainly seen as wage earners but the socialists of the nineteenth century had little interest in any input from women.

To say that someone is a moral person is to say that they are a human being with certain capacities. Usually, those capacities include an ability to make and act on individual decisions. The status of moral personhood is particularly important in certain political and legal contexts. Children, for example, often are not considered moral persons because they are not considered capable of making an independent judgment about right and wrong and then acting on that judgment. So, where 'human' is the metaphysical category (that is, the category of beings to which someone belongs), 'moral person' is the normative category to which rights, privileges, and responsibilities are usually accorded.

Women as rational and autonomous

Mary Wollstonecraft (1759–1797) was an eighteenth-century feminist who argued both for the full humanity of women and for the moral personhood of women. Her monumental work, *A Vindication of the Rights of Woman* (1792) advocated the equality of the sexes and responded to many who had argued otherwise. Wollstonecraft was an ardent spokesperson for social justice and human rights; she published many books before her untimely death (and is also known for her famous daughter, Mary Shelley, the author of *Frankenstein*).

Wollstonecraft argued for the rational humanity of women in *A Vindication of the Rights of Woman*. Secondarily, of course, she argued for the civil and economic rights of women. According to Wollstonecraft, human beings are characterized by reason, virtue, and knowledge. Reason is what distinguishes human beings from the 'brutes' or other animals. This was and still is a common conception of human beings: that we are creatures endowed with reason and it is that faculty which makes us superior or more divine (think of Augustine and how the rational mind might be directed toward God). Virtue, moral goodness or character, is what distinguishes one human being from another. Wollstonecraft is clearly leaving open the possibility of degrees of excellence – differences which mark some humans as superior to others. Her point, however, is that being born female does not in and of itself determine one's virtue. Finally, knowledge is gained through experience but if one's experience is circumscribed by social mores, then one will be unable to perfect one's nature. Happiness is dependent upon the perfection of nature. As you can see, Wollstonecraft set the stage for showing that the social dictates that keep women from gaining experience and advancing knowledge, keep them from happiness. Moreover, she argued that the 'feminine virtues' praised so highly by Rousseau and others of the day were merely rules of propriety. Women were taught to be elegant rather than virtuous and hence destined to be inferior.

Women were discouraged from developing powers of reason and thus lacked the virtue that society valued for full participation in citizenship. Wollstonecraft also reasoned that by excluding women from the development and practice of rationality, women were being treated as less than human. Her primary solution was to provide real education for women. She argued that women must act autonomously to be fully human. But she also argued that wifely and motherly duties were among the commands of reason and ought to be executed faithfully. An equal education that afforded women ample opportunity for rational and moral development would, according to Wollstonecraft, result in marriages characterized as companionship between equals. Friendship, rather than social status, would be the measure of success in marriage as a woman could be a friend to her husband and not just a pleasing ornament in his home. Nevertheless, although women and men have the same kind of intellectual abilities, they do have some differences according to Wollstonecraft and those differences are perhaps most apparent in their familial roles.

> One of the compelling arguments in *A Vindication of the Rights of Woman* compares the life of women under the constraints of social propriety with the life of soldiers: 'Like the *fair* sex, the business of their lives is gallantry. They were taught to please, and they only live to please. Yet they do not lose their rank in the distinction of sexes.'

Wollstonecraft seems to exalt reason and some later feminists find fault in that. They argue that Wollstonecraft was adopting the masculine model of personhood. Suggesting that women can fit that model and ought to be given the social and educational resources to allow them to fit that model appears to exalt men by making women more like them. Emotion, at least, appears to be put aside in favor of reason. But perhaps that is too simple a critique. Perhaps we ought not to accept that reason and emotion are themselves mutually exclusive. Some recent work on feminist ethics and epistemology (which I will discuss in Chapter 4) tries to recover the importance of including emotion in conceptions of personhood.

Another prominent twentieth-century feminist who promoted first wave ideals is Virginia Woolf (1882–1941). Woolf's book *A Room of One's Own* (1929) is an exploration of the hindrances a woman would face in seeking education on a par with a man at a prestigious university. Originally given as a series of lectures on women and fiction, Woolf asks her reader/listener to imagine what it would be like to walk across the great lawns and dine in the great halls of Oxford or Cambridge (referred to as Oxbridge). She invites us to think about a female Shakespeare – his fictional sister – to discover the encumbrances that would have prevented her from fulfilling her talent as a writer. A woman in Shakespeare's time was barred from lectures and libraries, publishers would refuse to consider her work, and social expectations would keep her from having long stretches of time within which to write.

Woolf asks quite explicitly what would be required for a woman to create a work of art. In answering, she takes her character to the British Museum in the hopes of finding the truth about women. There, she discovers the huge number of books of every genre written about women – mostly by men. Men of every ilk had answers for 'why are women poor?' These books purported to explain women's lack of virtue, lack of intelligence, and physical inferiority. Woolf's witty account of this foray into the literature on women highlights the lack of knowledge – but no lack of opinion – on the subject of women's inferior social status. They all failed, of course, because they began with the assumption that women are inferior and their books were filled with anger. The anger comes at least in part from the struggle to maintain superiority. Men, according to Woolf, have used women as a sort of mirror to reflect themselves back in grander terms. That is, through the admiration of women, men felt themselves to be better than they actually were.

Woolf forecasts a time when women would no longer be the protected sex, even predicting that within a hundred years of her writing women would be soldiers and laborers just like the men of her day. Her point was that gender roles are variable according to social values and that the assumptions about the sexes would change or disappear when traditionally male social roles are opened to women. Women will participate in all manner of activities, Woolf predicted, and the 'truth' about women's inferiority will fall away. The 'protected sex' is, in effect, protected from exercising liberty. Woolf famously argued that in order to write fiction – and indeed in order to participate in social life as men do – a woman needs 'a room of her own' and ample money to support herself.

As we have seen, Mary Wollstonecraft argued that women needed liberty in order to develop their rationality and moral virtue. In a similar way, Virginia Woolf highlighted the many obstacles standing in the way of women's intellectual achievements. Both understood humans to be autonomous and insofar as women were kept from acting autonomously, by custom or social mores, they were treated as less than human.

To be autonomous is to be 'self-legislating.' In a broad sense, that means that one makes rules for oneself but it is commonly understood to mean that one decides for oneself what one ought to do in all things big and small. Feminists like Wollstonecraft and Woolf illustrate how the social expectations, laws, and economic structures keep women from acting on their autonomy. So even while they argue that women ought to receive the same education as men to prepare them for full participation in social life, Wollstonecraft, Woolf, and others recognize the need to change other systems as well.

Social and political rights

Other rights that usually are not codified into law are social rights. By this I mean the category of rights that contribute to the general structure of society. The family is the most prominent element of social existence for the majority of any individual's life. Family structure says quite a lot about who is valued, what is valued, and how society as a whole is or should be structured.

The word 'patriarchy' means 'rule by the father' but it has been used to describe both rule in the family and political rule. Robert Filmer's (1588–1653) book *Patriarcha* (1680) defended the divine right of kings and argued that descent is through the fathers of families who have political power over wives and children in their families. While this stands as a sort of classic example of patriarchy in political theory, the term is used colloquially to mean that the men have the say in family life. The first of John Locke's (1632–1704) *Two Treatises of Government* (1689) is a response to Filmer and an attempt to argue for the equality of all people. Even in familial rule, Locke rejects the sole authority of the father, arguing instead for 'parental power.' Although he has been faulted for inconsistently holding this position, Locke's work does challenge us to rethink the traditional family structure.

In political theory, the relation between the family and society is often characterized by one of two general models. The first sees the family as a microcosm of society. The second views the family as a distinct society within the larger society. As a microcosm of society, the roles in the family are reflected in the larger political realm. This reflection might be a result of societies having their roots in extended family groups. Political power in the larger society is modeled on the distribution of power in the family (in its extreme form, this is patriarchy but there are much milder forms as well). The second model views the family as a distinct society with distinct systems structuring it and the larger political society.

These different conceptions of the relation between the family and society have tremendous implications for women. If the family is a microcosm of society, and if the family is patriarchal in structure, then society will be patriarchal as well. Women's roles in such a society would likely be limited to those that pertain to mothering or draw on the skills a mother might exhibit such as early childhood educator or nurse. The social roles that involve political decision making or ruling of any sort would likely fall to men. If, on the other hand, the family is a discrete society within a larger society, then a woman might still be subject to patriarchal rule (depending on how her particular family is structured) or she might enjoy a degree of relative liberty. That is, her role in the family would be separate and distinct from her role in society. A hazard of this second model of the family/society relation is that when the family is viewed as a separate society it has its own set of laws or rules and the larger society or state is cautioned against interfering. It is under just such conditions, when the family is understood as sacrosanct, that women are most at risk for abuse.

This discussion reveals another central aspect of first wave feminism: citizenship. Since ancient times, citizenship has been almost the exclusive province of males. At various times, certain women might have enjoyed that status of 'citizen' or even become rulers, but they are the exceptions rather than the rule. In philosophy, citizenship generally means membership in a political community. To be a citizen means one has certain rights and responsibilities that pertain to the proper functioning of the community. The rights usually include different forms of protection (such as protection of property, protection of one's person, and protection of privacy), liberties, so long as these liberties do not infringe on the rights of other citizens (such as the right to speak freely, the right to gather with others, and the right to practice one's religion), and the right to participate in government according to the specific system of rule (so, one may vote or run for public office in a democracy). The responsibilities include respecting the rights of others and doing one's part to maintain and sustain the community (like paying taxes and obeying the laws).

To be a citizen, in short, means being recognized by one's community as someone who matters – someone who is worthy of protection and trustworthy with responsibilities. Women's exclusion from the role of 'citizen' is very illuminating. No doubt one reason women have been excluded is that they were not always viewed as fully human as we have seen. But another reason is because they were not considered trustworthy or worthy of protection. The feminist movement has consistently worked to change that. In the first wave, the primary emphasis is on arguments to attain the same status as men. In subsequent waves, different approaches were employed. Feminist social philosophers and legal critics have argued that patriarchal notions are embedded in our conception of autonomy, rights, and citizenship. In that case, rights would have to be radically reworked or the very notion of rights abandoned and replaced with something else (perhaps relational theories such as care and solidarity) in order to bring about the type of social change that would liberate women.

John Stuart Mill (1806–1873) was a utilitarian philosopher, a member of the British Parliament, and the first person to speak in such an official capacity for the right of women to vote. Utilitarianism is a moral theory based on the idea that the best thing to do in any given situation is that which will bring about 'the greatest amount of good and the least amount of pain for all concerned.' Extending the rights of citizenship to women would, according to Mill, maximize utility.

Mill was extremely close with another prominent feminist of the nineteenth century, Harriet Taylor (1807–1858). They became friends in their early twenties and were philosophical partners throughout their lives. Harriet was married to John Taylor when she met Mill but, nevertheless, they fell in love. The Taylors already had three children and Harriet maintained at least the semblance of her marriage to John Taylor. He died in 1849 and two years later, she married Mill. Mill credits her with a great deal of his thought in his most famous feminist tract, *On the Subjection of Women* (1869), as well as some of what appears elsewhere in his social and political theory.

Some general aspects of Mill's thoughts regarding women might be focused into three basic categories: intellectual, economic, civil. Mill argues that women have not achieved the success that men have and thus appear less intelligent than men not because women have a different moral or intellectual nature than men but because women have had fewer opportunities and an inferior education. He notes that women have fewer experiences and less time than men. Those limitations alone mean that women would not be able to participate in the arts and sciences at the same level as men. Mill also claims that women have little desire for the celebrity or fame that comes from great accomplishment. So, just as Woolf used the idea of Shakespeare's sister to suggest that women's opportunities rather than their natures made them inferior, Mill blames the limited educational opportunities given to women for their seeming inferiority in society. The only way to discern whether men and women are by nature equal, according to Mill, is to give women equal education.

In economic matters, Mill held that women must be given equal opportunity in the public sphere. That is, women must be given access to all jobs. And in the civil sphere, he argued that women should have a voice in the formation of policy and law. True to his utilitarian philosophy, Mill outlined the possible benefits if women were given equality in education, civil life, and economic opportunities. First, he suggested that equality in social life would ensure that the relation between a man and a woman would be more just. In other words, Mill thought that social changes would affect the courtship and marriage relations between men and women, and that women would be less likely to be subject to the unjust dictates of a spouse. Second, Mill noted that opening the intellectual, economic, and civic roles to women would effectively double the available talent in service to humanity. The third notable benefit of gender equality is that the happiness of women themselves would increase tremendously. Liberation of women is consistent with the utilitarian purpose, maximizing the pleasure and minimizing the pain for all in society.

Clearly, Mill held to an ideal of marriage as life among equals. Even when some decisions needed to be made and one or other of the spouses took the lead, it would not establish any sort of permanent rule in the home. Children would similarly be raised valuing equality among men and women. Mill did quite a lot to advocate for the liberation of women but while he wanted women to have access to the same opportunities as men, he also thought that wives should not have to work. It was enough that the option to work be available to her. Similarly, the choice of whether to marry or not needed to be a true choice; without an ability to provide for herself economically, the choice to marry could only be a coerced choice based on financial necessity or social custom. Mill was a well-known advocate for birth control and also suggested that men and women marry late in life, have children late, and live in communities with extended families. These measures were to decrease the likelihood of divorce and to provide some stability for the children should there be a divorce. The extended community would remain a constant in the child's life even if the parents separated.

Harriet Taylor also wrote about the condition of women and advocated measures to ensure social and political equality. Like Mill, she argued that inequality between the sexes was due to society's customs and traditions. But unlike Mill, she advocated that women needed to work outside the home so that they would enjoy a partnership in economic matters. Taylor also argued that women must have the opportunity to remain unmarried (and equal footing in the economic world is required for that to be a real possibility). In contributing to the family financially, women would have more of a co-equal share in family decisions. However, revealing her class bias, Taylor argued that the family ought to get servants to do the domestic work while the wife works outside the home. Should the couple divorce, the woman should assume full responsibility for the children. As a way to alleviate the possible burden under such a plan, Taylor argued that women ought to have fewer children. Finally, Taylor also recognized the need for women to participate equally with men in shaping law and policy in the public sphere. But, of course, in order to do that, women needed to have their voices heard and in modern democracy that power is most easily recognized in the ability to vote.

These historical voices continue to echo in feminist efforts all over the world. Mill, Taylor, Wollstonecraft, and Woolf, each in their own way, were seeking to obtain social recognition that women are fully human and worthy of all the rights accorded to that status.

Opening legal rights for women: the vote

Some of the most public feminist campaigns have been efforts to bring about legal reform. Among the most prominent of those are the right to vote and hold public office, the right to speak in public, the right to make a contract, the right to own property, and the right to protection of person. But other laws and legal reforms are also necessary to facilitate the liberation of women. Among the targets for feminist legal reform are those laws that alter society's expectations of a woman as wife and mother. Laws regarding the family had to change to protect women and allow them to hold property or inherit wealth, among other things. In Europe and the United States, some of these laws began to be proposed in the eighteenth and nineteenth centuries but it would take until the twentieth century for women to truly be considered legal persons worthy of state protection against violence and to own and transfer property. Other legal reforms would also have to be addressed in order for women to participate in political and economic life equal with men. For instance, a change in the divorce law to allow for women to seek and obtain a divorce signals an equal recognition of women in marital relations; a change in laws covering the workplace to allow for maternity leave demonstrates at least some acknowledgment that childbirth is a difficult process but it also indicates a social recognition that women ought not to be penalized for giving birth (which itself is often seen as service to the community); and laws regarding the provision of early child-hood education help free women with very small children from the demands of domestic life.

The legal reform that, perhaps more than any other, makes the most difference in how women are perceived and treated socially and politically, however, is the right to vote. With the right to vote, women can more readily bring women's concerns to public and policy discussions and advance the emancipation of women and other oppressed groups.

But women's claim for the right to vote is met with quite a lot of opposition around the world. Some argue that women's views or opinions are already included in the vote of their husbands. Giving women the right to vote is simply superfluous. Moreover, allowing women to vote is an implicit acknowledgment that they might disagree with their husbands. At risk, some anti-suffragists argue, is the very fabric of the family. The Catholic Church actually favored granting women the vote in 1919 because Pope Benedict XV thought women would be a powerful religious conservative force in public politics. But his motive was politically pragmatic rather than feminist (he wanted to win back the balance of power in Italy). Another argument against allowing women to vote is that such participation in politics would sully the character of womanhood. Engagement in politics is a dirty business and when women – at least middle class women – are held up as models of moral rectitude, voting can only be seen as a bad thing. Feminine charm, it seems, requires women to stay at home and care for domestic things rather than become embroiled in politics. And, of course, building on the issues already discussed in this chapter, if women are not seen as fully human or lack an education equal to that of men, then they would not be considered qualified to vote.

In the United States, the women's suffrage movement grew out of and alongside the abolition movement in the nineteenth century. Among the many arguments women gave for why they

ought to have the vote was that women had a right to participate in economic and political life equally with men and having
a vote is the only state-recognized way to do that. More importantly, feminists like Elizabeth Cady Stanton used the
Declaration of Independence to support the cause for women's
enfranchisement. Stanton believed that all individuals are
endowed with inalienable rights by God; among those rights is
the right to vote.

But the suffrage movement is not without its problems.
Stanton is often criticized for not supporting the Fifteenth
Amendment, which gave blacks and former slaves the right to
vote. This criticism is not incorrect but it is only part of the
story. While many in the suffrage movement thought her
position was racist and unfaithful to the abolitionist cause,
Stanton was angry that the Fifteenth Amendment seemed to
legitimate the subordination of women. She was less interested
in denying the vote to blacks than in ensuring that women too
were included in groups granted the right to participate in the
republic through suffrage. Many suffrage fighters sought to link
the cause of women with abolition by rejecting measures that
only granted rights to some.

In making a plea for legal equality, at least some white
women compared their work in the home to slave labor insofar
as it was uncompensated labor. Women were often assumed to
be included in the property of the male homeowner but analo-
gizing their situation with that of slaves overlooks the often
violent situation of slavery. The situation of the slave was of a
categorically different kind than the situation of white, middle-
class suffrage movement feminists. Slaves were often separated
from their families, forced to have children against their will,
raped and beaten by the slave-owners, and regarded as chattel or
property.

Although women in the United States obtained the right to
vote in 1920 and women in Britain got some partial right in

1918 and rights on a par with men in 1928, there are still women all over the world who continue to fight for their right to vote. The United Nations recognized the right to vote as a human right in 1948 but even then women were not always included in the interpretation or understanding of that international human right. The specific acknowledgment of the right to vote for women did not come until 1979 with the Convention on the Elimination of all Forms of Discrimination Against Women (CEDAW). But, there is no world government to enforce human rights within nations. Women's suffrage is still denied in some countries and global feminists acknowledge that the right to vote ought never be taken for granted – in too many places and too many times women have been physically barred from casting a ballot and women's right to vote has been legally denied.

Economic rights

Taylor and Mill introduced us to some of the prominent issues pertaining to equal economic rights for women. Subsequent feminists offered arguments for the right to equal opportunity in employment, just compensation and comparable worth, and wages for housework. In a chronological account of the waves of feminism, most of these issues in the West fall in the second wave. But since we are using the thematic interpretation of the waves, these economic issues belong in the first wave.

Equal opportunity in employment simply means that women ought to have the same chance as men to obtain a job and advance through the ranks of that job. Until fairly recently, women were not given the same opportunities in many fields and there are still instances of gender discrimination that plague the workforce. We can look at equal opportunity as a three-step process. The first step is to remove the explicit barriers that keep women from getting good jobs. Employers used to be able to discriminate on the basis of sex in hiring and promotion. In the United States, Title VII of the Civil Rights Act of 1964 made that illegal. The second step is to weed out those subtle forms of discrimination that may abide by the letter of non-discrimination laws but not the spirit. For instance, jobs that specify certain weight or height requirements may intend to bar most women from qualifying. The third step is to change the attitudes or cultures of the workplace. If employers and fellow employees act in a sexist or harassing manner, then those actions may inhibit a woman's ability to succeed or even apply for promotion. Similarly, if fellow employees view one of their newly hired colleagues as an 'affirmative action hire' they may presume that she or he is less qualified to do the work. While this is a faulty inference, it nevertheless reflects an oppressive workplace culture that needs to be changed before women can enjoy full equality on the job.

As we saw in Chapter 2, Marxist feminists and socialist feminists both address the oppression of women as rooted in the material conditions of life. This is decidedly different from liberal feminists' claim that it is legal inequality that causes the oppression of women. Nevertheless, these different schools of feminist thought do share some common goals. One of those is just compensation and comparable worth. Just compensation means that women ought to be paid the same as men for doing the same job. Comparable worth means that women ought to be paid the same as men for doing comparable work. Both Marxist feminists and liberal feminists would also add that we need to systematically adjust wages in jobs that have been traditionally gendered. In other words, those jobs that have been traditionally held by women (elementary school teacher, day care provider, nurse, to name a few) are often underpaid because a 'woman's wage' was viewed as supplemental to the main income of her husband/provider. Even bracketing the fact that not all women have providers, the discrepancy in pay between men and women effectively means that women work for about a quarter of the year for free while men receive compensation throughout the entire year. Depending on the profession, socio-economic circumstances, and other cultural factors, the discrepancy can be even worse.

Well-known contemporary American feminist Gloria Steinem also notes that in order for women to truly have equal opportunity in the workplace, in addition to the access to jobs and adequate pay for all jobs (including the bad ones), workers also need to have some flexibility in their work schedules to allow for those times when family commitments pull one away from a nine to five job. Steinem also argues that married workers ought to share equitably in the parental responsibilities.

> In a brief flight into fancy, Gloria Steinem asks us to imagine 'What would happen ... if suddenly, magically, men could menstruate and women could not?' Here is an extract from her witty response:
>
> 'The answer is clear – menstruation would become an enviable, boast-worthy, masculine event:
>
> > Men would brag about how long and how much.
> > Boys would mark the onset of menses, that longed-for proof of manhood, with religious ritual and stag parties.
> > Congress would fund a National Institute of Dysmenorrhea to help stamp out monthly discomforts.
> > Sanitary supplies would be federally funded and free.'
>
> *Ms. Magazine*, October 1978

Another issue regarding economic rights for women, which also touches on the relation between family and society, is whether women ought to be paid for housework. Whereas most liberal feminists argue that some sort of sharing of childcare and cleaning duties will adequately free women from the role of primary domestic worker, Marxist feminists look for changes in how the capitalist system values and relies on domestic workers.

In 'The Political Economy of Women's Liberation' (1969), Margaret Benston argues, following Friedrich Engels, that we need to scrutinize the role of women under capitalism. Women appear to be a separate class, a class that is both required and exploited by capitalism. Benston defines women as people producing use-values in the home. A use-value is the value of products for immediate consumption that satisfy desires. It is the value of a product for the owner. Women create a number of 'products' in the home in the form of meals, clean laundry, healthy spaces, and other amenities. Homemakers also provide necessary emotional support that allows the worker to go out into the workforce every day. But, of course, women create this use-value in the home without any sort of compensation. Benston argued that household work ought to be converted into public productive activity. In other words, she advocated for the industrialization of household work.

In many ways, this proposal has a communal appeal and in many ways we have already taken steps to industrialize or social-ize housework. The communal appeal may be seen in the idea of expanding the unit of consumption. If neighborhoods or communities, rather than private families, share meals together or arrange living quarters around a common kitchen, then there are more opportunities for communal engagement and perhaps more collective sentiment and emotional support. Daycares and schools, take-out meals, cleaning crews, and even maintenance or construction crews are examples of some of the ways we currently share household tasks that were once solely the responsibility of the private family. Most of these are not social-ized in the economic sense; that is, most are not state sponsored services. But some might be. The state does provide free educa-tion and transportation to that education for children from the age of five to the age of eighteen in the United States. Other countries have even more expansive social services such as healthcare and elder care. The point is that Benston's proposal may at first strike us as impossible or at least too radical but it is not merely the stuff of science fiction.

Benston also points out that the structure of the traditional family, with female homemakers, turns those women into consumers for the capitalist system. As she puts it, by lacking an identity in the home, women become consumers in search of that identity.

But perhaps the most important aspect of capitalism's reliance on homemakers is that the large population of unemployed people create an army of reserve labor. That keeps wages for workers low, according to a Marxist analysis of capitalism, and also creates a demand on the workers to provide for all those members of the household who do not provide for themselves in the form of wage labor.

Like many feminists, Benston proposes that liberation for women is contingent on the access to jobs outside the domestic sphere in addition to the socialization of housework. Childrearing too should be shared by everyone in society and shouldn't just be the responsibility of individual parents.

In a similar vein, Juliet Mitchell argues that the division between work and family is deceptive. Work and family are interlinked, especially in the lives of women and children. Children learn what it means to be a member of society in the family. Gender and class roles are all first taught there. But whereas Benston argued that women's use-value was exploited by capitalism, Mitchell focuses on women's lack of time to participate in the exchange-value of capitalism. In other words, Mitchell is less concerned about the work women do to sustain workers in the home and more concerned with women as workers. Her argument for equal opportunity for women rests on this understanding of the exclusion of women from the workforce. Mitchell provocatively argues that the liberation of women must be pursued simultaneously with the liberation of the working class and vice versa.

A third view of women's work in the home comes from Mariarosa Dalla Costa. In her essay 'Women and the Subversion of the Community' (1971), Dalla Costa argues that women's work in the home is the central focus of women's role in society. She undertakes an analysis of housework in order to show that it is, contrary to Marx and orthodox Marxism, socially productive work. Dalla Costa asserts that women in the home are isolated but that in fact all women are housewives, even those who work outside the home. Women are called upon in the public realm of production to act the domestic roles, to maintain relationships and clean up messes. Unlike many of the feminist theorists we have discussed in this chapter, Dalla Costa focuses on the working class housewife. This focus reveals the way capitalism creates the role of housewife and exploits it beyond the home. The work that women do outside the home is linked to the work that is done domestically (as we saw also above with those jobs identified as traditional women's work). The work that women do in the domestic sphere is nevertheless invisible to society and not included in social production (or a country's gross domestic product). What is visible is the product of the domestic work: the children and/or the laborer.

But Dalla Costa does not advocate that work is the means to women's liberation because in the capitalist system work is still exploited. Instead, she argues that women's emancipation must occur in the family. Dalla Costa supports a rejection of the entire structure of housework. Women, she argues, need a new identity not associated with domestic chores. She thinks that paying women to do housework would only further cement the 'institutionalized slavery' of domestic labor. As might be expected, Dalla Costa also envisions a more complete struggle with the working class to overthrow capitalist structures; 'wages for housework' would not provide the sort of reform that is necessary. Hence, work too is not an adequate solution to women's oppression because work participates in capitalism; one would be throwing off one form of exploitation for another. Instead, Dalla Costa proposes the destruction of the housewife role and a revolutionary struggle for liberation with the working class.

These three approaches to the wages for housework proposal suggest some of the difficulty in bringing about real social change. The issues are all interconnected and often affect not only our communal relations but our personal identities as well. That explains at least some of the differences among feminist theories: feminists approach a particular issue from different vantage points. Even though all feminists share the goal of women's liberation, they often envision divergent paths to reach that goal.

THE GLASS CEILING

The glass ceiling is an invisible barrier that keeps women from advancing to the top rungs of business, academics, politics, and other fields. The 1970s metaphor illustrates the continued struggle for rights for women. The ceiling is formed both by overt policies that keep women either from positions or tracks where advancement is possible, and by subtle, covert assumptions about women's capabilities that block advancement. A liberal feminist might propose legislative measures to ensure equal access to good jobs and advancement within those jobs. A Marxist feminist might suggest a challenge to the capitalist class structure that relies on women to be underpaid or unemployed. A socialist feminist might suggest that the interconnections between race, class, and gender are all built on pernicious dualisms, which stand as a sort of unifying concept of oppression. Other feminists would look to further causes for the injustice and suggest additional solutions to liberating women. But in spite of these differences, feminists share the similar goal of emancipation.

Human rights

Countless contemporary feminists work tirelessly for women's rights. Indeed, feminism itself is often associated with equal

rights for women, with the effort to obtain and maintain reproductive rights often in the forefront. These rights give women
some freedom to decide when or whether to be pregnant.
Catharine MacKinnon, however, challenges us to go back to the
first question of this chapter with the title of her book *Are
Women Human?* (2007). At root in this question is whether
women have human rights or are protected by human rights.

Human rights are generally understood as universal obligations humans have to one another. The United Nations
Universal Declaration of Human Rights (1948) is the most
widely accepted account of human rights and the first article of
that document asserts the freedom and equality of all human
beings. Nevertheless, the UN Universal Declaration of Human
Rights may be faulted for its Western bias – even the language
of 'rights' reveals a particularly Western orientation to obligations we have to one another as humans. And many nations do
not agree on some of the provisions spelled out in the document
because those provisions are contrary to cultural beliefs or
practices. The UN Universal Declaration of Human Rights is
problematic for women because it is not yet the case that
women are understood as fully human or worthy of human
rights protections in all nations, and women do not yet share
equal political status with men throughout the world. In
addition, it does not address issues that are specific to females.
MacKinnon argues that violations against women are often
overlooked; they are not deemed violations of women's human
rights but gender specific issues. The challenge, then, is to get
the UN and the entire international community to recognize
gender specific issues such as rape as worthy of human rights
attention.

At the urging of feminists and women's activists all over the
world, the UN has issued a number of subsequent documents
and covenants that attempt to address gender specific issues. The
UN Declaration on the Elimination of Violence against Women

(1993) explicitly aims at extending the rights enumerated in the UN Universal Declaration of Human Rights to women. Global feminists continue the cause for women's human rights by building coalitions among feminist groups across borders and seeking common goals for further alliances.

One example of feminist efforts to obtain human rights and also acknowledge the gendered nature of a violation is in the activism surrounding female genital cutting, also called female circumcision or female genital mutilation depending on the position one takes. Female genital cutting (FGC) actually encompasses a variety of practices classified by the World Health Organization into four basic categories. The first is the removal of the clitoris or clitorodectomy. The second is the removal of the clitoris and the labia minora (and possibly the labia majora). The third form includes these excisions and also sews up or seals the vaginal opening. This form is called infibulation and leaves only a small hole for urine and blood to pass through. The WHO's forth category is a sort of catch-all to account for other forms of ritual genital cutting such as piercings which may or may not include the removal of flesh. All forms of female genital cutting are cultural rituals performed on girls ranging from infancy to adulthood, but most commonly between the ages of five and thirteen. Those who argue that genital cutting is a violation of human rights stress that it is often done without the consent of the girl or woman and often in unsanitary conditions. They present it as an act of violence against women which is also frequently indicative of a wider lack of respect for the human dignity of women, hence the name 'female genital mutilation' which distances this act from male circumcision. Activists opposed to FGC hold it up as a gross violation of the rights of women. In particular, FGC violates the rights of bodily integrity, sexual expression or pleasure, and security in one's person. It is also said to leave countless psychological scars in addition to the physical ones.

Nevertheless, FGC is not uncontroversial within feminism. Some cultures defend it – with the support of women – as a traditional practice with significant meaning. Even some feminists defend the practice saying that those opposed to it are imposing their own cultural values or particular conceptions of human rights. Those who defend FGC highlight the rights to freedom of religious and cultural expression and argue that while some female genital cutting is performed under unsafe circumstances, most of it is not.

This debate illustrates some of the difficulties that accompany many efforts to obtain full protections of human rights for women. Rights sometimes conflict and the gendered nature of some acts can make efforts to bring about change much more complicated because the issue or act is not considered a matter for human rights talk, because women are not the subjects of human rights, or because of conflicts between cultures, traditions, and approaches to justice – the very nature of human rights is, after all, rooted in a Western liberal tradition.

Another contemporary situation that draws the efforts of feminists interested in human rights issues is the French ban on religious apparel and other symbols in schools. This ban, which was found to be in accordance with human rights by the European Court of Human Rights, is meant to support a sort of secularism that it is believed contributes to a sense of national community. But the ban poses an undue burden on Muslim girls and women who choose to or are instructed to wear the head scarf as an enactment of their faith. Worn in school, the scarf has been judged to be in violation of the ban even though small Christian crosses are allowed. The justification hinges on what are perceived to be obtrusive symbols of religion, symbols that would disrupt social cohesion or distract from school lessons. This issue brings to light issues of sex and gender inequality but it also might be seen in light of France's colonialist past.

Feminists concerned about human rights emphasize the confluence of issues here. On the one hand is the right to freely express one's religion in public or private so long as doing so does not threaten the rights of others. A ban on apparel that appears directed primarily at Muslim girls and women does not seem to be upholding the right to freely express one's religious beliefs. Nor does it seem to treat everyone equally given that its effects are most evident on school girls. But on the other hand is the right to equal protection and security in one's person (especially in educational settings) and the state's obligation to carry that out. If France understands religious symbols as posing a potential threat to an individual or a group, and views a ban on such symbols as the best way to protect those individuals, then it might be argued that the state certainly has a right to enforce the ban even if it appears to target Muslim girls. Moreover, feminists are divided about whether the head scarf and other forms of veiling are themselves indicative of sexual inequality or are otherwise demeaning of women. Some argue that the head scarf or veil is freely chosen and even empowering insofar as it protects women from at least some of the objectifying gaze of males. Others argue that the veil is a symbol of women's subordination and lack of autonomy in some cultural and religious traditions.

Regardless, the feminist efforts to secure human rights internationally, in spite of difficulties determining what that would mean, are important extensions of feminist efforts to secure the legal, social, political, and economic rights of women within one's own nation.

Women have made tremendous gains all around the world but there is still more to accomplish. Women are still more likely to be victims of violence, women still disproportionately care for infants and children, and women are still underpaid compared to their male peers. Some of the changes in legislation now need to be backed up with cultural changes that affect how laws are implemented. In addition, not all of the manifestations of oppression can be remedied through changes in legislation, the structure of the economy, or even social and political transformations. Oppression is often internalized – incorporated into how one thinks of oneself and others. Second wave feminism analyzes some of the ways oppression is structured beyond inequality. In the next chapter, we see how oppression affects agency, identity, and embodiment as well as feminist proposals to change how we act, how we think of ourselves and others, and how we experience our bodies in the world.

4

Expanding the sphere of influence: the second wave

As we have seen, the first wave of feminist activism may be characterized by struggles to gain recognition of the legal, economic, social, and intellectual status of women. The second wave might be understood as trying to address all of those aspects of women's oppressed experience that are not addressed once legal, economic, and intellectual equality are achieved. In part, this also means refining what we understand as equality but it also extends to women's bodily experience in culture and society. Changing the laws prohibiting women from entering the workforce does not always change the way women are treated once they are part of that workforce. Granting women full rights of citizenship with the right to vote does not always mean that the specific concerns of women will be heard or that women will be taken seriously as participants in political life. By adding an analysis of oppression that extends to understandings of the body, morality, subjectivity, and identity, second wave feminism allows additional means for understanding and combating oppression as well as further requirements for liberation.

The Second Sex

The woman most frequently credited with bringing in the second wave of feminism is Simone de Beauvoir (1908–1986).

Beauvoir was one of the twentieth century's leading intellectu-als and her book, *The Second Sex* (1949), was an unprecedented study in the cultural myths, social standards, and life situations of women. She uses existentialism, a philosophical movement popularized in France in the twentieth century, to frame the question: 'What is a woman?'

Beauvoir develops an account of existential ethics in *The Ethics of Ambiguity* (1947), and uses that as her methodology in *The Second Sex*. Freedom is the central value and every project that an individual undertakes should in some way embrace freedom and open up more freedom for oneself and others. Another way to think about this is that each person creates him- or herself by acting in the world. If a person acts in a way that closes off freedom, then he or she becomes more like an object than a person. For instance, if a person chooses be a housewife and then lets that role determine her choices such that she no longer acts like a free being, then she has closed off freedom. Of course, sometimes the social situation may close off freedom first. Beauvoir exposed the many ways that women's situations circumscribe their ability to act freely.

The oppression of women differs from other forms of oppression like racism or classism insofar as there appears to be no historical starting point – women have always been oppressed. When social roles require women to be wives and mothers, they live and work in isolation. That precludes at least some of the possibilities for solidarity. There is no solidarity of work interest because women are in separate households and there is no solidarity of location (as might be found in ghettos) for the same reason. In fact, women often have more in common with the men of their social class than with other women. That makes collective efforts for liberation much more difficult.

Beauvoir's purpose in *The Second Sex* is to promote liberation for women but she shows that liberation is a very complex achievement. The book is broken into two parts; the first part explores why women are oppressed. She looks for the answer in all of the places that other people have suggested – historical materialism, biology, and psychoanalysis – but finds that none really answers the question accurately or completely. Instead, she argues, women's whole situation is oppressive: an array of factors converge to create the unique situations in which individual women find themselves. The second part of the book provides an account of women's situations.

Beauvoir also reveals the cultural myths that surround women, motherhood, feminine sexuality, and other aspects of women's lives. She analyzes history to see how women have been treated and what attempts have been made to free women from oppressive conditions. In addition, she offers a study of literature to show how symbolic portrayals of women become not mere representations but standards by which real women are measured.

Woman has been defined as Other, according to Beauvoir. Men are the One or the norm and women are the Other because they are both similar to and different from men. Like men, women are human beings with freedom who are also subject to nature. That is, human beings are natural beings – they have bodies which are often unpredictable or uncontrollable. Desiring to be free and create their own meaning in the world, men fear this nature; and as a way to attempt to control it, they make woman the embodiment of nature through myth and custom. Men create the cult of the 'feminine' or the 'feminine mystery' to maintain the oppression of women. Women are taught how to be as women, i.e., passive, object-like, free beings mystified into believing that they are confined to particular 'natural' roles which limit freedom. So, a girl is raised to believe that her destiny is to be a wife and mother and that she will experience satisfaction in these roles. Her freedom or her ability to act on her freedom is truncated.

Beauvoir uses the concepts of 'immanence' and 'transcendence' to further explain women's situation. Immanence is stagnation and immanent activities endlessly repeat the mundane (like dishes that once washed will get dirty and need to be washed again). Transcendence is reaching out into the future through projects that open up freedom (like a profession that continually opens new possibilities). Although every human being is both immanent and transcendent and must participate in both sorts of activities, some social practices may seem to imprison one in immanence such that one is unable to achieve transcendence. That is what happens in every case of oppression. Women's oppression relegates them to the sphere of immanence while men occupy the sphere of transcendence insofar as they work on meaningful projects that reach into the future. Beauvoir refers to the start of the menstrual flow as a reminder to the girl of her immanence. Menstruation is a monthly reminder of her attachment to the body as servant to the species via reproduction. This (among other things) marks women as 'natural' or subject to the vicissitudes of their bodies in a way that men are not.

Beauvoir also argues that women are complicit in their own oppression; that is, women internalize the consciousness of the male gaze and the expectations of gender roles. Women measure themselves and each other according to socially constructed and variable standards of beauty, behaviour, activity, and sexuality. Beauvoir refers to the 'eternal feminine' as the perceived essence of femininity that all women are supposed to have according to societal myth. Of course, as an existentialist, she believes that there is no such essence at all. Rather, women and men adopt the myths as reality and criticize each other harshly for failing to live up to the myths.

Beauvoir's famous line, 'One is not born, but rather becomes, a woman,' serves as a central point for the *The Second Sex*. It marks the shift from her description of the cultural myths to the analysis of the situation of women. She argues that each woman will actually inhabit a unique situation that is composed of her childhood experiences, her relationship to her own sexuality, the social milieu in which she finds herself, and cultural marital habits or expectations. Although in childhood boys and girls appear relatively equivalent in their freedom, in adolescence girls realize both the fact that they are free and that their oppression sets up a situation wherein acting on that freedom is nearly impossible. This causes the crisis of adolescence, according to Beauvoir. The frustration of being unable to act on freedom may continue into adulthood or a woman may resign herself to the roles prescribed for her.

Liberation is both an individual transformation and a social transformation. Woman must see herself as subject like man, and not object. She must embrace her freedom and embrace projects that further disclose freedom. But women must also see themselves as a social group. Failing in this assists in maintaining the oppression; women must recognize the unity in shared circumstances of oppression, they must, in other words, recognize the mystification of the eternal feminine.

Beauvoir suggests four strategies to aid women in their path to transcendence or subjectivity: (1) women must go to work; (2) women must pursue and participate in intellectual activity; (3) women must exercise their sexuality in freedom; (4) women must strive to transform society into a socialist society and seek economic justice.

By describing in vivid detail the countless ways that women experience the limitations of femininity Beauvoir opened the way for women all over the world to recognize the social and political importance of personal experience. Her book ushered in a new wave of feminist activism because she had the courage to make women's social, familial, bodily, political, and cultural experiences public. She wrote about things that had heretofore been taboo subjects and she spoke with a clarity and honesty about women's bodies and sexuality that many still find shocking even sixty years after the publication of *The Second Sex*.

Although some people question whether women are still the 'Other' that Beauvoir describes, we can continue to gain valuable insights about the structure and content of oppression from reading Beauvoir's analysis of women's situation.

> 'Representation of the world, like the world itself, is the work of men; they describe it from their own point of view, which they confuse with absolute truth.'
>
> Simone de Beauvoir, *The Second Sex* (1949)

In a similar way, Betty Friedan's (1921–2006) highly influential book *The Feminine Mystique* (1963) is credited with enlivening the feminist movement in the United States. Friedan identified something she called 'a problem that has no name.' This problem was characterized by the general malaise that many women felt in their middle-class homes. They had been raised to believe that they would find satisfaction in being a wife and mother but, instead, they often felt depressed, lonely, or generally dissatisfied. Friedan began her research for this book by conducting a survey among her 1942 graduating class from the all-women's Smith College in the US. Although her sample population was seriously limited, the themes she explored in her book awakened a movement: many women realized they were not alone in feeling dissatisfied with familial life and written off by society. Friedan advocated that women ought to go out and work. She argued that the stifling life of a housewife was the root of the problem – not some mysterious feminine ailment that only psychoanalysis could uncover. She pushed for a different way to view the family and a different social existence for females.

Sex versus gender

Many feminist theorists read Beauvoir as articulating a distinction between sex and gender. Such a distinction was employed in a great deal of feminist theory from the 1960s to the late 1990s and is still very useful in some contexts. 'Sex' marks the biological categories that are presumed natural, given, or obvious. 'Gender,' on the other hand, indicates the social categories. So, while 'male' and 'female' designate biological sexes that are distinguished by their roles in reproduction, 'masculine' and 'feminine' name social categories that are culturally specific, change over time, and include a wide array of characteristics and roles. Take something like body image as an example. What is considered feminine in one society at one point in time may be quite different from another society. Social expectations or cultural mores for hairstyles, clothing, comportment, even average bust and hip sizes of women seem to fluctuate dramatically within any given society. These are a result of social conventions or socially constructed expectations of femininity; they are the traits of gender.

This sex/gender distinction includes a number of implications for understanding the oppression of women. First, when gender is understood as a social construct, then much of women's oppression shifts too to being understood as a product of society rather than being grounded in the nature of females. In some ways, that makes the situation much more hopeful. If social practices define woman in such a way that individual women are unable to practice self-determination or pursue freely chosen projects, then changing social constructs of gender might alleviate the problem. If women are naturally inferior to men, then feminist efforts to change unequal social relations would be futile. But if any inferiority is the result of perception or variable gender roles, then feminists working for social change can actually accomplish equality between the sexes.

Second, gender as a social construct allows feminists to conceive of political unity among women. Here the idea is that by sharing similar experiences of oppression or similar gender expectations, women will find commonality among themselves and unite for political action. During the second wave, consciousness-raising groups were frequently used to capitalize on the revelation about the social construction of gender. I discuss this particular social and political feminist strategy in the next section on sisterhood.

Gender as a variable social construct also implies that one can be a female but not be a 'woman' or a male and not be 'man.' Indeed, biological males could choose to adopt feminine gender characteristics and biological females could adopt masculine gender traits. A person might even opt to mix a variety of gender traits. If gender is a social construct then recognizing its pliability means opening the possibility for all sorts of combinations of gender traits.

Some feminists question the strict division between sex and gender however. Perhaps biology too is also socially constructed in various ways. Even Beauvoir, and Friedrich Engels before her, noted the effects of social activities on the body. Perhaps the notion that women have different muscular-skeletal structures is itself a result of social conditioning that gets reinforced through breeding and is passed down from one generation to the next. For instance, women are often said to be physically weaker than men. If biology is a social construct like gender characteristics, then women's physical weakness would be attributable to a long history of limited physical activity. The muscle groups essentially disappear though genetics and natural selection. Further, intersex individuals – people born with ambiguous genitalia or more than just XX or XY chromosomes – might be seen as proof that there are not two sexes but many sexes. Intersexuality is obscured by the socially constructed binary between biological male and female.

A related issue pertains to whether there is anything essential about being a 'woman' at all. Some postmodern feminists suggest that 'women' do not exist because there is no essential characteristic or even essential experience that all women have.

In other words, they argue that the word does not refer to a metaphysical category because there is no defining feature of that category. Such a position could be useful in challenging sexist conceptions of women because it denies they have any relevance – they do not refer to anyone. But many feminists also find the denial of the category 'woman' troubling because it appears to take away the possibility of a group that might wield political power for positive social change.

There is likely some middle ground here between saying that women do not exist and saying that gender is still an applicable category describing a social construct. Some feminists argue, for instance, that 'woman' is and will remain a valuable category insofar as there are political reasons for it. When some people are targeted for exclusion, marginalization, or violence on the basis of sex or gender categories, regardless of whether those categories are perceived, natural, or socially constructed, then there is still some use for categories like 'woman,' 'gender,' and, of course, 'feminism.'

Sisterhood

The debates over sex and gender tend to work their way back to the possibility for collective feminist action. Many political movements seek to build solidarity among participants. Beauvoir called for solidarity among women in strategies for liberation that touched off the second wave. Solidarity comes in many forms however. One model is 'sisterhood.' Sisterhood is a notion of unity among all women, that is, that all women are sisters. But what makes women sisters?

One idea is that sisterhood is founded on shared experiences of oppression. Women might bond over our shared anxieties, sufferings, and trials. Think, for example, of an average plane flight. With the exception of a few pleasantries exchanged here and there, most passengers of any given flight do not feel any particular relationship or bond to all the other passengers. That changes, however, if something happens on the flight. Suppose there is a lot of turbulence, so much that the flight becomes difficult or frightening. Or suppose the plane blows a tire on take off and it becomes uncertain whether it will be able to land safely. Might these difficult, dangerous, or scary conditions cause the passengers to unite in more substantial ways? The more difficult the situation through which people endure or survive, the more likely people will reach out to each other in some way or at least feel connected simply because they shared an experience. Sisterhood is a bond similar to these experiences. Perhaps women share a bond or seek to connect with other women because they relate over the difficulty of their experiences of being subordinated, the victims of violence, stereotyped, excluded, or otherwise oppressed. Women who work in an office where there are clearly sexist practices that adversely affect them might commiserate with each other and that could certainly build and extend well beyond the office itself.

There are a number of strengths to grounding sisterhood in shared experiences of oppression. First, it helps to name a problem. Sexual harassment was not identified as a problem until women started sharing their experiences in the work force and feelings of aggravation, irritation, or misery. In fact, it was not until the late 1970s that sexual harassment was formally recognized as such. Women talking with women and sharing experiences played a large role in bringing it to public consciousness. Similarly, domestic violence, date rape, and gender discrimination all gained prominence once the experiences moved out of the private lives of individual women and were recognized as social problems.

Another strength of the sisterhood approach to bonds between women is that as women share an experience of violence or oppression they might also gain feminist consciousness.

Consciousness-raising groups of the feminist movement began as relatively small groups of women sharing their personal stories. They quickly developed into more formalized mechanisms to support other women. The groups also offered information and educational resources – these services were particularly important for helping women who were victims of sexual harassment or domestic violence to navigate through the social and legal systems that would help remedy their unjust situation.

There is also the personal benefit that comes from sharing one's story and realizing that one is not alone in the experiences of violence or oppression. When women are sisters they support each other and share an understanding – often unspoken. In other words, sisterhood implies moral and epistemological bonds between women regardless of whether individual women actually know one another. The idea is that all women are subject to sexist violence, marginalization, exclusion, and by virtue of this subjection, women are united. Sisterhood should mean that sisters aid their sisters in need. But, of course, women do not always or even often respond in compassionate ways to other women. Sometimes, women even blame each other for the violence they suffer – as when a woman says of a friend, 'why doesn't she just leave the abusive relationship?' or 'if she hadn't dressed like a slut, she wouldn't have been raped' and similar indictments of each other.

Sisterhood is also problematic in a number of other ways. Not everyone actually shares the same experience of oppression. If feminist organizing relies on a bond among women and that bond is grounded in a shared experience of the same oppression, and if there is no shared experience of oppression, then no bond will form and feminist organizing will be paralyzed. Moreover, any number of particular circumstances may affect how a woman experiences oppression. Take the case of sexual harassment as an example. A woman in a white collar, high paying job who is sexually harassed in the work place probably has access to lawyers, counselors, or psychologists to help her maintain her self-esteem and combat the injustice. A woman in a low paying job that requires little trained skill will, in contrast, likely fear for her own job security and may hesitate to even report the harassment. She also would not likely have the disposable income to spend on lawyers and psychologists. If she chose to report her experience, she would have to rely on the good will of her employer – which is often absent, or if he is the harasser, impossible – and if the case went to court she would likely have to rely on legal aid or pro bono assistance if she was able to obtain it. Strategizing for feminist activism given such widely divergent experiences of oppression is very complicated. It is complicated even further when we realize that much of feminist theory and activism itself emerges from middle and upper class women and men. Some feminists might not even understand the complexity of problems facing women outside their class and race background.

Another serious problem with sisterhood is that it tends to emphasize victimhood. Certainly naming and identifying a problem shared by others is important. Many women find the initial experience of consciousness-raising quite empowering. Nevertheless, focusing on the many ways that women are victimized can be all-consuming and quite paralyzing. If sisterhood stops at how women are victims together then they never get to the point of changing the social and political systems that cause that victimization. Women have to move beyond being victims in order to identify the many strengths women have and act on those strengths for the good of all.

Identity politics

Some second wave feminist social and political theory capitalized on group affiliation based on shared identity for understanding both subjectivity and solidarity. Identity politics was a reaction to the solidarity or sisterhood grounded in shared experience as well as a further attempt to obtain social, legal, intellectual, and economic rights for oppressed peoples. Rather than assuming that all women have the same experience of oppression, feminist proponents of identity politics seek representation of diverse identities (or diverse experiences of oppression) within the larger society. Generally speaking, identity politics is a movement or trend in social and political theory. The 'identity' is a shared identity based on cultural background, linguistic community, ascribed identity (that is, other people labeling some people as part of a group), or other shared experience of oppression. Since different groups experience different forms of oppression, they would likely develop different identities. More specifically, identity politics means that there are a wide variety of different forms of oppression, which in turn create a variety of different needs. The political system is thus charged with recognizing these diverse groups and their needs. A 'politics of difference,' to borrow from the title of Iris Young's 1990 book, is a politics that is able to practice recognition, validating the diversity of identity and experience while also listening to the individual groups' expressions of needs.

Identity politics challenges traditional social and political theory because in recognizing differences between groups, public policy must treat individual people differently. The political community must ensure that the structures of democracy weigh the needs of oppressed peoples heavily in order to overcome the long historically entrenched disadvantages and oppressions which neglected those needs. In other words, identity politics encourages special recognition of how oppressed group identity has shaped individuals and continues to adversely affect their ability to participate in and be treated with equity in social life.

When contrasted with a traditional social and political theory, such as social contract theory, the effects of identity politics can be seen quite clearly. Social contract theory assumes more or less equally situated, equally talented, and equally treated rational individuals. Identity politics opens political theory to new and challenging ways of incorporating differences and reconceiving equality as something to be achieved rather than assumed. Moreover, it assumes that people have to be treated differently given certain social differences. Identity politics is often understood in popular culture as representation of diversity within politics. For feminism, one way it is manifest is when women are elected or appointed to public office. The expectation is that by virtue of being a woman, the elected official will represent women's concerns. The problem is that people do not often or even usually think of themselves as members of identity-based groups.

A feminist proponent of identity politics might cite Margaret Thatcher, the first female Prime Minister of Britain (and the first female leader of the Conservative Party), as an example of getting women into political offices. She clearly broke some very durable barriers and she is frequently held up as a success for women generally. Of course, Thatcher also famously said 'I owe nothing to Women's Lib.' Her legacy for women is contested ground. Certainly her mere presence as Britain's highest political figure challenged assumptions about women's capabilities and potentially opened doors for other female politicians. But her work while in office is often portrayed as damaging to women's place in society and she did nothing to advance any sort of women's cause. In effect, this reveals a hazardous side to identity politics: that it is a mistake to assume that because one has an identity one will act on behalf of others who share that identity. India's first female Prime Minister, Indira Gandhi, held the office from 1966 to 1977 and again in 1980 until her assassination in 1984. Her tenure as Prime Minister is controversial for numerous reasons but she did act with concern for the poor and underprivileged of India, explicitly including women and children in her efforts. Of course, she also repudiated the label 'feminist' on numerous occasions but in doing so was distancing herself from the feminism of the US which she described as striving for women to mimic men.

Extreme forms of identity politics assume that having a woman or an African American or any other member of an oppressed class in positions of power would make a difference. They are no doubt correct about that – the public presence of successful people from oppressed groups is very empowering to members of oppressed groups and helps to change dominant perceptions as well. A flaw enters into the reasoning when it is assumed that an identity necessarily determines one's political commitments. While it may be the case that a person's identity determines or at least contributes to the political issues one pursues in public office, it is not a necessary relation. So, while identity politics has tremendous potential in empowering and representing groups, it does not necessarily follow that it will transform the public and political landscape so as to alleviate or remedy oppression.

Identity politics has also been critiqued for proliferating identities. If identity groups are the foundation for political representation, then relatively hard lines need to be drawn between identities. In practice, that is nearly impossible to do. Races are not clearly differentiated and individuals may in fact identify with multiple races. In such an instance, how do they get represented? Similarly, if women are a group, then the diverse circumstances of race, class, sexual orientation, disability, and gender are overlooked or obscured. That obscures what issues ought to be brought to public or political discussion and often entrenches systems of class or race domination while attempting to obtain representation on the basis of sex.

Race and class

Identity politics raises an important issue characteristic of second wave feminism: ought women to be treated differently or the same? The issue is really twofold. First, the equality/difference dichotomy refers to whether, in seeking equality, women seek sameness with men or different recognition given women's unique capacities. Second, the equality/difference dichotomy pertains to the metaphysical question about the nature of women: are all women essentially the same or are there important differences between women?

The discussions of sex/gender and sisterhood above reveal some of the strengths and weaknesses of equality understood as sameness; the discussion of identity politics helps to illustrate some of the strengths and weaknesses of focusing on difference. Although there is no feminist consensus on how to resolve these issues, there is general recognition that such things as race, class, sexuality, and disability ought to be included in feminist theorizing.

In the last three decades, critical race theorists have raised the question 'what is race?' In doing so, they challenged the understanding of race as a natural category. Race as a natural category implies that peoples of the same race will share at least one characteristic in common – and are usually perceived to share many. In a racist society, one of the characteristics would be a natural or inherent inferiority. The white social biologists of the early twentieth century, for instance, sought a biological basis for the inferiority of blacks. By dismantling the biological bases for race, critical race theorists destroyed the naturalistic foundation for social inferiority. Moreover, race became a political category rather than a natural or biological one. In a racist society, the people in power or the people who are privileged by the racist system largely determine the political category of race. Anti-black racism, for instance, entails violence and unjust stereotyping of blacks as well as granting unearned privileges to whites. Feminism may find commonality between sexism and racism or feminism may find that it participates in racism or benefits from it.

Class oppression poses a different sort of problem for feminist theory and for liberation theory generally. One's class status is often presumed to be a result of one's own efforts (or lack of efforts). This is certainly true for some people but the majority of us owe our class status to inflexible social structures that open doors of opportunity to some and put up barriers to advancement for others. Class status becomes all but unshakeable. Even when a person is able to climb up the social ladder, certain marks of lower class status might remain. Vocabularies, tastes, school pedigrees, fashion sense, and other aspects of one's public presentation may belie roots in lower classes and may prove to inhibit one's ability for further advancement. Among other things, this example reveals that class is not just an economic status but also a social status or social mark. The challenge for feminists is to understand how class affects or impacts sexist oppression and what sort of issues a feminist theory attuned to class ought to make central.

Initial attempts within second wave feminism to recognize the effects of racism and classism on the lives of women offered a sort of building block approach. Each new form of oppression was stacked on to others. Occasionally, arguments would break out as to what was the most damning form of oppression or who had it worse off. But ultimately, the building block approaches are unproductive. They encourage competition among those who struggle for liberation as each group draws on limited resources and compares their own situation to the situation of others.

Alternative models invoke the language of 'intersections' or 'interconnections' and I apply these to some issues in Chapter 7. Intersectional thinking comes from Kimberlé Crenshaw's work mentioned in Chapter 2. Crenshaw shows the short-sightedness of thinking in terms of only race or gender, and the limitations of thinking in a building block manner. By thinking about the intersections of forms of oppression we are able to see some of the aspects of oppression that affect women because they are 'black women' and not just because they are 'black' and 'women'. This sort of intersectional thinking moves beyond the proliferation problem of identity politics by emphasizing the failures of social and political theory and praxis rather than the race, class, and gender identities.

Public existence and the private sphere

Second wave feminism popularized the expression, 'the personal is political'. The message of this rallying cry was that women have suffered in private as individuals but refuse to any longer. The 'personal' includes those things one experiences as a female body as well as those things that one experiences as a woman in the home and workplace. Menstruation, pregnancy, childbirth, housework, rape, domestic abuse, sexual harassment, and count-less other topics were brought out of the private realm and into public discussion. By politicizing these things that essentially had been hushed up, feminists expanded the understanding of oppression. Women's bodies and homes, not just women's social and political existence, are recognized as the sites of oppression. In this way, feminists blow apart the oft-used distinction between a public life and a private life.

When used to describe the distinction *between* the domestic sphere and civil society, the dichotomy of the public and the private relegates women to the private sphere and sends men out into the public. In this case, the private is generally indicative of some notion of family. The public is the realm of all that is not private, i.e., the public is politics, the military, employment, and everything else that does not constitute domestic life. Because the spheres are set up as mutually exclusive, there exists the possibility that each sphere is governed by different principles. Second wave feminism specifies that what is at issue is that women are largely excluded from the public sphere where decisions that affect their lives are made. This leaves issues such as spousal and child abuse out of public discussion and attention; the 'sanctity of the home' protects actors from unnecessary intrusion but it also blocks protection against the private harms in the home. Feminists propose alternatives that validate the domestic realm as worthy of public attention or that deny there can be a strict split between public and private. Some suggest incorporating the principles of the public into the private, others have suggested the converse.

The split between the public and the private is also used to distinguish types of activity into production versus reproduction. Productive activity is activity that creates surplus value for the state (the public sphere). Reproductive activity creates use-value or value for immediate consumption within the home. Reproduction includes childbearing and rearing, as well as domestic labor, and caring for elderly parents. Marxist and socialist feminists note that women's reproductive labor is not acknowledged within the capitalist system. They seek ways to make the personal political by either bringing reproduction into the realm of productive labor or otherwise ascribing a productive value to reproduction, or destroying the sharp distinction between production and reproduction entirely.

In addition to the various dichotomies of the sex/gender distinction (masculine/feminine, male/female, man/woman), the public/private dichotomy, and the production/reproduction split, second wave feminist social theory scrutinized other dichotomies to see whether or how they might play a part in the oppression of women. Dichotomies are ways of categorizing thought into two mutually exclusive categories. The problem is that the two categories rarely operate on an equal plane – one is understood to be inferior or undesirable while the other is superior and valued. Moreover, numerous feminists have noted the effects of dichotomous thinking on women. Women are usually associated with the inferior, subordinated half of the dichotomy. This can be seen quite clearly in the culture/nature dichotomy.

Man creates culture through reason and artifice, whereas woman, whose primary role is to give birth, is associated with nature. Feminist theory has to disrupt this dichotomy. It does so in varying (and at times contradictory) ways. One way to challenge the split is to show the many ways women contribute to culture. Another is to argue that childbirth is not merely or even primarily a 'natural' process. Other approaches deny that there is such a strict division between culture and nature or suggest that man-made culture is nothing really to be proud of. Perhaps the most longstanding challenge to the dichotomy is found in ecofeminism (discussed in greater detail in the next chapter). Ecofeminism and other ecological movements reclaim the value of nature for Western thought.

Psychological oppression

Sandra Lee Bartky argues that woman's oppression infiltrates one's psyche to become 'psychological oppression.' She shows that women are stereotyped, culturally dominated, and sexually objectified in ways that fragment and mystify them. Other feminists and other oppression theorists have also discussed the internalization of oppression that shapes a person's consciousness, understanding, and knowledge. Bartky is illustrative of this strain in oppression studies and captures a great deal of insight from feminist efforts to expand the conception of oppression, thereby expanding what is required for liberation.

Stereotypes are generalizations about a group. Individuals identified as members of the group may have nothing in common with the stereotype of the group but are nevertheless measured and judged by it. According to Bartky, stereotypes fragment women by reducing them to parts. One woman is reduced to being a wife rather than a person with multiple interests and pursuits while another becomes merely a prostitute without understanding her dreams or what led her toward that profession. Stereotypes limit a person and become internalized such that the woman who is reduced to being a wife measures her self-esteem according to only that part of herself. In a similar way, stereotypes mystify. Mystification is when a person comes to believe that the stereotype is natural; reality becomes mixed up with the oppressive psychological messages according to Bartky. So the wife or prostitute in the examples above comes to believe that she obtains her role because she is naturally destined to it or for some self-deprecating reason.

Cultural domination, according to Bartky, is similar to the culture/nature dichotomy discussed earlier, but rather than associating women with what is natural, cultural domination minimizes women's cultural contributions and excludes them from the primary realms of cultural production. Fragmentation and mystification are found here too. Bartky argues that language, art, cultural institutions such as universities, and literature are sexist. Language is a particularly apt example. Using the male pronoun when the gender of the noun is unknown can be internalized. Girls who grow up hearing about firemen and mailmen, or who always hear doctors referred to as 'he' may not consider that those professions are open to them. But Bartky's point moves even beyond these rather obvious examples. She shows how culture not only reflects sexist ideas or attitudes but also how it actively sustains and maintains the exclusion or marginalization of women and other oppressed groups. Fragmentation occurs because women are cut off from cultural contributions – their creations are considered craft rather than art, their writings are overlooked in the curriculums of universities, and their literature with women-centred or feminist themes is deemed not rigorous enough for the standards of culture. Mystification creeps in as women accept these assessments of their cultural contributions, believing that women are not able to succeed on a par with men.

The third element of psychological oppression is sexual objectification. Sexual objectification occurs when a person is turned into an object for sexual purposes. Beauty pageants have been the target of feminist activism for just this reason. Bartky emphasizes that a woman's sexual parts or abilities are objectified for instrumental purposes. A woman becomes a womb or a cunt. She is reduced to her sexual parts and represented by them. That in itself is fragmentation. Mystification adds to the psychological oppression because she internalizes the objectification and believes that she is no more than a sexual object for use by men.

BRA BURNING: FACT OR FICTION?

Feminists are often stereotyped as 'bra burners.' This stereotype is rooted in a feminist protest of the 1968 Miss America Beauty Pageant. Activists had a 'Freedom Trash Can' in which they threw bras, girdles, pots, pornography, and other 'instruments of female torture.' Nothing was burned – not even the bras!

Psychological oppression affects differently situated women in different ways. Some women command more social status and are able to overcome a good bit of the mystification even if they are still fragmented by the gaze of others. So too, other forms of oppression often intersect with sexism and cause different forms of stereotypes and sexual objectifications to combine with or overpower the sexist ones. Nevertheless, internalized or psychological oppression is a significant force in the lives of oppressed peoples and liberation strategies must have some tools in their arsenals for overcoming it.

Feminist ethics

In traditional ethics, the focus has been on the definitions of and relations between terms such as justice, the good, autonomy, rights, obligation, moral agent, and responsibility. Notice, however, that these concepts generally pertain to individuals as moral agents acting independently. Feminist ethicists address these and similar concepts – often modifying them to incorporate feminist insight – but also add issues concerned with the relationships between ethical agents as well as the social roles or expectations attributed to gender.

Normative moral theory – be it traditional, feminist, or contemporary non-feminist – is charged with prescribing behavior. The aim of a moral theory is to provide the moral actor or agent with action-guiding principles that cover both positive and negative duties, i.e., what ought to be done and what ought not to be done. Feminist normative moral theory accepts the additional requirement to incorporate the experience of women. Thus, while striving to achieve justice for women, feminism provides a new perspective of the human being as an ethical agent, a new way to participate in or conduct human activities, and a new way to think about what is the subject of ethical discourse.

A feminist ethics will likely challenge or change how we understand 'autonomy' or 'justice' in order to be more inclusive of some of the things that characterize women's experiences. When we understand autonomy, for instance, as an isolated individual making decisions solely for him- or herself, we fail to see the way relationships affect decision making. Autonomy can be reworked to include that relational aspect or it may need to be abandoned in favor of a more fluid, communal concept. Similarly, justice might be transformed from abstract fairness to concrete social justice in response to the recognition of personal interconnections – especially with the most vulnerable among us, such as children.

Community plays a significant role in feminist moral theories. A feminist analysis calls for a recognition of the interconnection between what happens on the local level and what happens on the global level. To this end, what counts as community becomes an important meta-ethical concern. First of all, community provides a forum for identity formation and is an integral part of full self-determination. The individual participates in a variety of communities thereby forming or defining them while they in turn also contribute to the individual's identity. Thus a moral theory must be able to account for both the individual and the social groups/communities to which the individual belongs. Second, the boundaries of community indicate the type of relationship and subsequent responsibility that many feminist moral theories use as a guideline for action. Community might be determined according to proximity of people, location, shared interest, or even physical attribute. There is no isolated individual or lone moral agent for feminist ethics.

Feminist moral theory emphasizes experience in two ways. The first is that moral theory and moral issues arise in response to the situation of individual men and women. Some feminist ethicists refer to the specific experience of women, while others emphasize the experience of all those who have been marginalized by traditional moral theorizing or otherwise excluded from the 'norm.' Still others challenge traditional moral theory to use actual rather than hypothetical experience so as to better confront lived reality. The key is that theory takes its guide from real experience and does not attempt to limit what ought to be considered appropriate for moral discourse.

Second, feminist ethics recognizes that theory is grounded in a particular socio-historical context. Acknowledging this opens the way for us to confront biases and critically evaluate the implications of a specific theory. This means that as times change our moral theory may have to adapt. It also links with the next meta-ethical issue, identity and difference, in that cultural differences assume an important role in moral theory as well as practical ethics.

Perhaps the most blatant way traditional ethics has failed women is by failing to see or account for women's concerns. Women's concerns were not considered philosophically interesting or worthy of deeper thought. Most traditional or canonical accounts of ethics claim that women's moral activity was confined to the home and ruled by nature or instinct. Occasionally, something like public opinion, taste, or the pursuit of beauty would be mentioned as playing some role in women's decision making but these were notably absent from the laudable forms of moral decision making discussed by canonical texts. In addition, some feminists have faulted traditional moral theory for being too heavily based on a conception of reason that excludes emotion. Regardless of whether these concerns are socially constructed based on gender roles or naturally determined, the work women do and the roles they adopt in society ought to be taken into account in philosophical formulations of ethics.

For some of the most prominent canonical moral theorists, such as Immanuel Kant and Jean-Jacques Rousseau, the principle object of man is to become more perfect as a citizen; the principle object of woman is to become more perfect as a wife. She was not considered an independent moral agent but was assumed in the moral agency of her husband or father. It is not surprising that the first major attempts in the Western liberal tradition to articulate a feminist ethics focused on assertions of a woman's full personhood and the development of universal virtue rather than a specifically male virtue or female virtue.

Mary Wollstonecraft, John Stuart Mill, and Harriet Taylor Mill each argued that moral virtue was not gender specific. Women had been relegated to a certain social role (wife and mother) but their ethical obligations ought to be determined in the same manner as the men's. Second wave feminist ethics takes a slightly different approach. Rather than adopt the masculine as the norm and argue that women are capable of fulfilling it, second wave feminists sought new sources for ethics that would be inclusive of women and women's concerns. For example, traditional ethics and politics emphasized the ability to take life in war rather than the ability to give life through birth. Recognizing the unique capacity to give birth changes how values are prioritized and decision making is structured.

There is, of course, a difference between a *feminine ethic* and a *feminist ethic*. A feminine ethic is an ethic that is grounded on special 'feminine' characteristics that women are said to possess. For feminine ethics, these characteristics or attributes are generally understood as the product of nature – part of the essence of being female – and might be used to support an argument that women are 'more moral' than men. For instance, a feminine ethics might argue that because women give birth to children they are inherently more peaceful. This could lead to all sorts of related conclusions about what roles women can and ought to play in social and political relations. Similarly, perhaps having the ability to give birth means that women are more nurturing. An ethics built on women's nurturing capacity would emphasize caring relationships rather than or in addition to fairness or justice. This approach falls under the broad category of an 'ethics of care' but very few care theorists actually hold that there is something innate about women that makes them more caring. So, the ethics of care might be either a feminine or a feminist ethics, depending on how the theorist explains the source of the caring disposition.

Alison Jaggar proposes that feminists must develop ethics from the understanding that the subordination of women is morally wrong and the moral experience of women is worthy of respect. She also asserts that feminist ethics is uniquely situated to bridge the gap between theory and practice, thought and action. The idea is that a feminist ethics would not only offer guidance in moral situations, it would also be guided by those situations. A moral theory is feminist in its methodology and content. The two are not separated or separable, though a theorist may focus on one or the other.

Ethics of care

By far the most prominent and perhaps the most controversial feminist ethical theory is the ethics of care. This normative moral theory sprung from the psychological research of Carol Gilligan and is often juxtaposed with a Kantian deontology or justice-based normative theory. Many feminist moral theorists have criticized traditional Kantian ethics for overemphasizing justice to the exclusion of responsibility grounded in relationships. In order to remedy this apparent problem with traditional Kantian ethics, many feminist ethicists have articulated an alternative that uses intimate relationships both as a model for moral obligation to others and as a starting point for decision making. Care within a particular context, rather than abstract principles of behavior, then becomes the guideline for ethical decision making.

Gilligan was a student of moral psychologist Lawrence Kohlberg, who developed a six-stage conception of moral development. Kohlberg's stages traced development from a punishment orientation wherein a child is obedient (or moral) because he or she fears punishment to the highest level of moral development in autonomously selected universal ethical principles. The lower stages all suggested that people are moral because they want to be perceived as good in the eyes of others – in other words, moral decision making was motivated by maintaining some interpersonal relationships or maintaining one's status as good in the opinion of other people. The higher stages emphasized abstract law or contractual agreements as the basis and motive for moral decision making. The highest, self-legislated universal ethical principles assume that individuals act independently but universalize the principles on which they act such that they would expect all other people to act similarly. The particular context of a decision or the relationships that it affects ought not to be part of the deliberation according to Kohlberg.

In studying these stages (which he developed by testing male subjects), Gilligan used the same moral dilemmas and scenarios that Kohlberg had used but noted that girls and women tended to respond by focusing on the relationships of the participants in a moral dilemma scenario. The boys, on the other hand, tended to focus on individual rights and the legality of the fictional scenarios. Boys viewed the actors in the dilemma as autonomous, independent individuals making moral decisions on the basis of reason alone. The girls viewed the various characters as interdependent subjects with a community orientation making moral decisions on the basis of emotion as well as reason. Ethically, this means that the boys tended to view the characters in the dilemma as operating according to abstract principles of justice. The girls viewed the characters as operating according to the importance of relationships and responsibility within those relationships. According to Kolhberg's six stages of moral development, females who made moral decisions in this manner were morally immature while males were at a higher stage of moral development.

Gilligan concluded that instead of women being morally immature, they simply tended to make moral decisions differently; her findings are presented in the book *In a Different Voice* (1982). Subsequent theorists have explored the cause of this difference in moral decision making. Some argued that the disparity is due to patriarchal socialization while others claimed it was due to women's innate capacity as caregivers. Whatever the cause of the 'different voice' women tend to exhibit in moral decision making, Gilligan's work has resulted in the theory called the 'ethics of care' and has altered how all moral theorists think about ethics.

Some care theorists posit that care comes from familial relationships, especially the relationship between mother and child. Others claim that women have a different way of thinking that informs a more caring approach to all forms of decision making.

Care theorists often suggest a web analogy to help illustrate how caring functions in moral decision making. Imagine a spider web. The different parts of the web are intertwined and reliant on each other. These different parts are like the people with whom we are connected. When an individual faces a dilemma, that individual does not just decide and act in isolation. Rather, that decision takes into account the many relationships one has with others – most of whom care for the individual too – and also has an effect on these others. Moreover, the decision itself probably involves the decisions of caring-others in its very nature and origin. Just like a spider web, some relations are more central to a person than others. Care theorists suggest that there is an ever expanding web of relations and most argue that the closest proximate relations matter more to decision making than the more distant ones. Some versions of the ethics of care also extend this web of relations to distant others either through the expanding web or through similarities between distant others and those one is close to. Ethics does not always pertain only to humans though. Some environmental ethicists have found the ethics of care applicable to the more-than-human-world – plants, animals, and whole ecosystems.

The methodology of care has been the subject of much debate and discussion. Caring is a very personal act done in a particular context. To create moral principles based on that seems counterintuitive. For this reason, care theorists eschew principles altogether. Instead, they offer guidelines for caring action. Among the many guidelines proposed are: (1) develop a 'disposition to care' which means that a moral agent has an attitude or desire to care; (2) act on a duty to 'care for' – care ought to be acted on appropriately and in a non-domineering way; (3) attend to the caregiver, or, make sure that in caring we do not exhaust ourselves or totally lose ourselves in those we care for; (4) pay attention to context and reciprocity. Caring is, in some way, exactly what a patriarchal culture asks of women so it is important that feminists not fall into the trap of validating feminine self-sacrifice while they attempt to reclaim the unique insights and contributions of women.

Like other normative theories, the ethics of care can be applied to any moral issue. Nevertheless, feminists tend to emphasize women's experience in developing the applications of an ethics of care. For instance, an ethics of care has been applied to the care of elderly parents, the care of the environment, domestic violence, childbirth and other biomedical practices, parent/child relations, and all of the many decisions that contribute to the raising of a child, business situations, and countless other moral situations.

For all of its strengths, an ethics of care is not without its weaknesses too. Some moral theorists – feminist or not – oppose any strict juxtaposition of justice and care; the two can and often do work together in different moral theories. Among feminists, some argue that an ethics of care is modeled on relationships that are perpetually imbalanced, unequal, and frequently unreciprocated: the parent–child relation. Other criticisms focus on the potential for self-sacrifice on the part of the caregiver, the possible abuse of caring, and the potential for caring to become oppressive or domineering. Another problem may be that an ethics of care does not have sufficient potential for collective political action or a strategy for liberation. Such a critique suggests that care must entail not only the specific relations in which it is evidenced, but must be politicized so as to acknowledge the ramifications of caring action on other relationships as well as oppressive structures.

Lesbian ethics

Other feminist approaches to ethics are more overtly political than the ethics of care. They might be based on something like existentialism, political solidarity, postmodernism, or radical feminist tenets. I discuss only one other explicitly feminist ethics – 'lesbian ethics' – here, but existentialist feminist ethics was represented by Beauvoir, ecofeminist ethics is discussed in the next chapter and global feminist political solidarity is presented in Chapter 6. Like an ethics of care and ecological feminist ethics, there are numerous articulations of lesbian ethics. All lesbian ethics theorists, however, agree that from their position on the margins of society, lesbian perspectives reveal the privileges of heterosexuality. Lesbian ethics is credited with highlighting the need for a feminist ethic to examine the institution of heterosexuality along with the examination of the family, marriage, work-place, etc. as subjects for ethical discourse.

Lesbianism is commonly thought of as an individual sexual preference or orientation. Lesbian ethics adds another dimension to this understanding. Accordingly, lesbianism also may be a political commitment, i.e., a commitment to put women first, which may or may not entail same-sex sexual relations. This is an important aspect of the woman's movement, although controversial in the mid 1970s when it was first proposed. Some radical lesbian feminists held that one had to be lesbian in order to be a feminist. But feminists from other schools of thought argued that it would hurt the feminist movement to enfold lesbians and lesbianism into its cause. (No doubt they were also concerned about fuelling the false stereotype that all feminists are lesbians.) The more moderate lesbian ethics position sees challenging the presumption of heterosexuality as useful to feminism because it simultaneously challenges gender roles. Lesbianism as a political commitment tells women that they do not have to derive their identity from men. Women could turn to other women for emotional support and escape entirely from the status as 'second sex' to men.

Because lesbianism was for so long shunned by Western culture, lesbians experienced invisibility as a group. It is precisely this experience of invisibility or marginality that gives rise to the insights of feminist lesbian ethics. Both sexual and political lesbians could critique traditional ethics as well as aspects of the feminist movement for not examining the oppressive structures of what Adrienne Rich calls 'compulsory heterosexuality.' According to Rich, women have been socialized within a patri- archal culture to be heterosexual (a quick look at the toys, books, and movies targeting young girls supports this claim). Rich argues that patriarchal socialization hides us from our true selves and encourages competition between women. Women need to create women's spaces or women centred culture to allow women to be free from these oppressive prescriptions and learn to be woman-identified. Lesbian ethics holds that it is only in this context, a woman-identified context, that one can truly be free to make moral decisions. Heterosexuality per se is not problematic; but the dominance and presumption of heterosex- uality as well as the social privileges that accompany it are. Patriarchal conditioning exclusively toward heterosexuality keeps women from being free according to lesbian ethics.

Certainly the consciousness-raising groups and efforts at sister- hood might be understood as attempts to create women's spaces. Some lesbian ethicists established retreat centers and communes to facilitate the break from patriarchal socialization. Among the many important contributions of lesbian ethics is the critique of feminist theories that unconsciously assume a heterosexual model. Lesbian ethics and third wave queer theory demonstrate the inter-sections and interconnections between sexism and heterosexism as forms of oppression. As society becomes more comfortable with social change and a non-exclusionary vision of social participation, these sorts of movements within and outside of feminism will continue to be very important in pushing us to greater under-standing of oppression generally.

Embodiment

Looking back over this chapter, one of the aspects of life that is most clearly central in second wave feminism is how a person lives in a body. Philosophers call this embodiment. Second wave feminists broke new ground in identifying the causes and effects of things like eating disorders, female sexuality, sexual violence, standards of beauty, and even bodily comportment. In Chapter 7 I discuss some of these topics within each of the different waves of feminism in order to illustrate the different approaches and methods. Here, I offer some thoughts about embodiment in general and its place within second wave feminist concerns.

In a way, embodiment has its roots in an age-old philosoph-ical problem: the relationship between the mind and the body. René Descartes famously examined this problem in the sixteenth century. According to Descartes, the body is a mere machine that is animated by the rational mind. Mind and body are two different sorts of substances – the mind is non-extended substance and the body is extended substance (it takes up space). Even in his own time, though, Descartes faced the problem of how to explain the interaction between mind and body. How, in other words, could something that does not take up space have any sort of impact on something that does? Subsequent philosophers have tackled the question and offered a wide variety of explanations. Although those accounts usually fall under the umbrella of the philosophy of mind, some feminist explanations have a distinct place in social philosophy.

Embodiment as a feminist concept pertains to how one lives one's body. Given that women's bodies are often the subject of much social control as well as the focus of uniquely female contributions to society, embodiment is the subject of both critique and positive theory construction.

Some feminists use embodiment as a way to critique social expectations of women. Eating disorders and plastic surgery, for instance, have both been presented by some feminists as resulting from women's alienation from their bodies. When society sends more or less consistent messages about what constitutes the ideal body or even the 'normal' body for women and men, then deviations from those norms may cause an individual to view her or his body as foreign or even the enemy. In an effort to seek control over this alien force, a person may resort to extreme measures such as life-threatening starvation or surgery. Notice how this conception of the body as alien or 'other' appropriates Beauvoir's conception of otherness. The Other is a threat that one seeks to control.

In a similar way, the body might inspire shame. As Beauvoir argued, menstruation has been mythologized in such a way that its onset might cause a young woman shame at being subject to the forces of nature. Patriarchal standards of feminine comportment might also contribute to shame of the body. A leering gaze or catcall might cause a woman to hide her breasts and legs, covering her body to avoid being objectified or reduced to its parts.

Of course, not every bodily experience results in alienation or shame and not every woman has an ambivalent relation to her own body. Embodiment is also simply how we experience the world. Descartes' question gets transcended: instead of 'how does the mind interact with the body?' it becomes 'how does embodied subjectivity interact with the world?' Shame and alienation seem to emphasize the reverse of this relation – how the world affects one's experience of the body. Instead of universalizing claims about the body, subjective embodiment seeks communicable experiences and empathetic understanding between and among subjects. Women experience their bodies differently at different times and in different contexts. By eschewing essentialist claims about how all women experience their bodies, subjective embodiment empowers women to think about how they live their bodies individually. This is leagues different from the medieval attempts to flee from the body or the modernist attempts to mechanize the body. The lived body shapes and is shaped by the world.

Feminist discussions of female sexual pleasure reflect the changes in how women experience embodiment. Sexual intercourse used to be understood in the Western world as defined by and focused on the activity of the male body. Sex was penetration and ejaculation. Women and women's sexual pleasure are almost entirely absent from such an understanding of sex; women who did seek or experience sexual pleasure might be vilified or filled with shame. They are there only to be penetrated and perhaps also impregnated. Some people even referred to women as mere vessels for reproduction, but recognition of a woman's own subjective experience of her body during sex was not part of the conversation. When the body is reduced to an object for reproduction, alienation often results. Second and third wave feminists have made huge strides in reclaiming sexual pleasure for women; teaching women about their own bodies, the multiple sites and sources of sexual pleasure, and female orgasms; and educating the public about equality and reciprocity during sexual intercourse. Third wave feminists also brought a larger discussion of autoeroticism and non-traditional sexual relations into the mainstream.

Finally, embodiment also has a metaphorical function. Political philosophers since Plato have used the body as a metaphor for the state. Body politics of this sort interests feminists both because the body represented is often a male body free from the natural rhythms and relationships often associated with women and because the state/body metaphor may be reversed to illustrate the shaping influence of power on the body.

The claim that the state is represented by the male body is multifaceted. It could mean any of the following (and probably more though also probably not all at the same time): (1) that the state is patriarchal; (2) that reason rather than nature ought to rule the state; (3) that only men are represented in the state; (4) that the state is phallocratic; or (5) that the values privileged in the state or society are masculine values.

Beauvoir hinted at the reversal of the metaphor. She suggested that the state could represent the body and thereby illustrate power to shape the body. The biological differences between men and women are not as crucial to how women are treated, as how those differences are interpreted by a culture or society according to Beauvoir. Subsequent theorists capitalized on this observation showing how such things as the popular media create women through the power of pervasive messaging. When confronted with images of how the body should be, people tend to respond by trying to conform. That is not unlike the coercive power of the state compelling people to conform to certain rules. Feminists like Bartky, using the work of French philosopher Michel Foucault, even talk of ways that the body is policed.

Clearly there are many ways that a person lives as, in, with, and through a body. Understanding how oppression affects embodiment moves feminist theory well beyond equality under the law toward a much more complex conception of liberation.

Religion

Earlier, we learned that Beauvoir uncovered some of the cultural myths that contribute to the oppression of women or otherwise define and limit women. Religion is perhaps the most prominent cultural use of myth. All three of the major monotheistic world religions – Christianity, Islam, and Judaism – struggle with ancient patriarchal traditions. Other religious traditions, notably Hinduism and Buddhism, also have elements of patriarchy, or what might be called sexist practices, but it tends not to be as embedded into the theological and spiritual beliefs as one finds in the monotheistic traditions. I focus only on the latter here. One of the central questions raised by feminist theologians is whether those patriarchal traditions are necessary to the belief and practice of religion. Two areas where this question is clearly visible are the representation of God and the leadership within religious communities.

God is represented in language as well as in descriptive accounts of God's nature. Judaism and Christianity both refer to God as 'Father'; Islam refers to God as Allah without gender. The name Father evokes the love and care of a parent as well as the power to make and enforce laws. It is a fairly explicit reference to patriarchy according to feminist theologians. Moreover, the language of worship is often masculine or makes use of the masculine pronoun in reference both to God and to believers. But God need not be represented solely as the male Father. Other words also describe the transcendent being and these alternatives may help to destabilize other patriarchal images. For instance, radical feminists suggest calling God 'Goddess' or 'Mother God,' ecofeminists sometimes use 'Creator,' and feminists of all sorts advocate referring to God as 'God' in all instances so as to avoid male pronouns entirely. Each of these alternatives connotes different images for God and also emphasizes different attributes of God.

Human knowledge of the attributes of God was a common topic of study in the medieval period but it has not lost its appeal, especially given feminist concerns about the relation between divine attributes and human attributes. When God is represented as being a strong, powerful law-giver, and men are perceived to be stronger and more powerful than women and also hold positions of authority in the home and the state, then the natural conclusion is that men are more like God than women are. Of course, there is a lot that may be said about this and feminist theologians have thoroughly refuted the argument on the grounds that God's attributes are not limited to those masculine characteristics, that philosophy and theology has been dominated by men who created an image of God in their own image, and that God ought not be identified (and limited) using essentially human attributes.

The major world religions are also patriarchal in organizational structure. Males not only dominate the leadership positions but also maintain a near exclusive hold on positions of power within institutional religions. Women have only recently been admitted to the higher realms of leadership and only in some denominations or sects within the major monotheistic traditions. For Christianity at least, the exclusion of women was justified on the basis of their difference from God and their association with more temporal, earthly, or bodily concerns. Like the exclusion of women from other areas of social life, the prohibitions against women holding positions of power in churches were often based on their childbearing capacities. Moreover, in Catholicism, for instance, women are barred from the priesthood because it is believed that Jesus selected only male apostles – this in spite of the fact that women were leaders in the early Christian Church.

Another element of the relationship between women and religion is what accepted or traditional theology says about women. All three of the major world monotheistic religions describe women's roles as primarily or solely pertaining to the family. Often they also include fairly explicit statements about the inferiority of women. In addition, they also include indictments of women's bodies. Women's bodies are a source of sin or temptation, they must be controlled or covered, and women's movements or locations in worship services must be curtailed. Such teachings regularly inculcate shame in women and encourage acceptance of inferior roles.

Feminist responses to the sexism in religion are creative, extensive, and variable. Most radical feminists reject the traditional religions outright. They hold that sexism is so inherent in Christianity, Islam, and Judaism that a woman cannot participate without being complicit in sexism. Some radical feminists have created new spiritualities and new religions or revived old non-patriarchal traditions to supplant the sexist institutions they leave behind.

Another feminist response, less radical perhaps but still quite challenging, is to attempt to reform institutionalized religion from the outside or from the inside. By either means, feminists employ social critique to unmask the contradictions in religious belief systems and reveal those sexist elements that are entirely superfluous to belief. They also work creatively to replace patriarchal images and language in the practice of faith and insert more women into religious rituals.

Standpoint epistemology

Standpoint epistemology is just one of many feminist theories of knowledge. I discuss a few recent trends in feminist epistemology and philosophy of science in the next chapter but I want to put standpoint here because it arises alongside identity politics and the ethics of care. Standpoint epistemology has roots in Marxist thought. Marx held that the engaged position of the

workers offered a clearer understanding of the system and structure of oppression – in short, a clearer picture of reality – than
the privileged capitalists who had no real incentive to scrutinize
societal structures. Nancy Hartsock suggested that feminists
adopt this strategy for articulating a feminist epistemology. She
argued that by looking at the material reality of women's work
in the home, we could discern a feminist standpoint.

The initial premise of Hartsock's standpoint epistemology,
like Marx's, is that there are two groups in opposition. For
Marx, the proletariat opposed the bourgeoisie. For Hartsock,
women oppose men. Importantly, however, neither theorist is
making any sort of essentialist claim about workers or women.
Both hold that it is the organization of society that has created
this opposition. The people in power, the bourgeoisie or men,
determine what is 'true' and set the standards for appropriate
sources of knowledge. But Marx and Hartsock argue that
through their struggles, the oppressed actually have a clearer
vision that discerns that the powerful simply determine standards
for knowledge and reality that maintain their position as powerful. The standards themselves are false or at least deceptive. In
short, the oppressed gain a vision through their work and struggle in a stratified society. Notice too that a standpoint is context
dependent; it is based in a time and place.

Because the division of labor is rooted in a sex division,
Hartsock analyzes women's work as both childrearing and
contributing to subsistence. Other differences between the labor
of women and the labor of men become apparent along this axis.
Women have a double workday. If they work outside the home,
they also face a disproportionate amount of work once they
return home. Women's work also tends to focus on use-value,
all the activities of reproduction rather than production. In the
shadow of Beauvoir, Hartsock points out that women's
work tends to be more mundane and repetitive than men's
while also taking away most of her free time. Notice that

women's work in reproduction is embodied. It involves both mind and body in a way that defies the dichotomy.

Other standpoint theorists have taken the theory in many different directions, developing black feminist standpoint and Latina feminist standpoint among others. Standpoint theory is not without its problems however. Some feminists are critical of standpoint's reliance on a binary between oppressor and oppressed. Others see the emphasis on work or activity as problematic. In addition, as we saw with identity politics, there might be a risk of proliferating standpoints such that everyone has a privileged understanding in relation to others on at least one point. Nevertheless, standpoint theorists can and have responded to these criticisms and the theory has gained significant ground in offsetting more traditional approaches to epistemology.

One of the chief insights from standpoint is the notion that norms for knowledge are socially constructed by the powerful as a way to maintain their status. The questioning of norms becomes a central theme in third wave feminism as well. I take up that topic, and many more, in the next chapter.

5
Language, thought, and cultural production: the third wave

Third wave feminism is greatly indebted to first and second wave feminism; it assumes many of the same struggles and also adds a new layer for feminist criticism. Some third wave feminists, drawing on postmodernism and deconstruction, reject 'theory' as too totalizing or universalizing. Theory might be replaced with narratives or new ways of writing but the idea for these feminists is to unsettle some of the metaphysical categories – such as 'woman' – upon which theory relies. Other third wave feminists embrace new forms of theory and new ways of doing feminism. Similar to the other waves discussed in the previous two chapters, not everyone who identifies as a third wave feminist agrees on the topics, issues, and methodologies that best advance the feminist cause and not every feminist I will discuss using this thematic approach to the waves would necessarily embrace any particular 'wave' designation. Nevertheless, there are common threads. In this chapter, I use the thematic organization to explore third wave feminist accounts of the structures of consciousness and language but I also present some of the new strategies for social change. Like first wave and second wave feminism, third wave involves some creative uses of culture in order to advance the feminist cause.

Methodology

The methods of third wave feminism are often quite different from second wave and at times there has been real animosity between second and third wave feminists. There is no consistent 'third wave methodology' but there are some definite trends. Four trends are: (1) multiplicity and the rejection of norms, (2) critique of the structures of consciousness, (3) use of popular culture, and (4) political coalition building in spite of ideological differences.

Third wave feminists embrace radical multiplicity even within an individual. Influenced by the postmodern and deconstructionist philosophers of the late twentieth century, postmodern feminists, for instance, reject an essentialist notion of self identity. The self is always changing or is never the same from moment to moment. Some draw upon psychoanalysis to substantiate this position and criticize phallocentric or phallogocentric culture.

Whereas feminism's first wave might criticize the unjust distribution of rights to favor men, and the second wave highlights other ways that society is structured to privilege men (and white upper class men in particular), feminism's third wave shows how even things that appear to be gender neutral (like notions of equality and freedom) might be built on structures of thought that are masculinist or male-dominated. When male dominance is embedded in norms, values, language, and consciousness, women's position as a subordinate class or caste might be hidden. The third wave endorsement of radical multiplicity attempts to get us not only to *think* differently but to *differently* think: to reject (or at least question) the singular way of thinking dedicated to phallocentricism and discover multiple ways of thinking, writing, and living in society in non-domineering manners.

This leads us to another common methodological thread within third wave feminism: the rejection of norms. We see this most clearly with sex and gender norms but it is also present in the rejection of standards or rules in sexuality, politics, ethics, language and writing, bodies, minds or consciousness, and desires. Norms try to impose an accepted and 'good way' of being in the world, participating in society, or living in one's body. Very often, however, norms inscribe oppressive identities on people who are 'on the margins' or who deviate from the norm. Second wave feminism, as we have seen, identified that experience of oppression; third wave feminism tries to turn the problem of norms back on itself, destroying all the limiting standards that put some people in the center while some are on the margins. In other words, by rejecting norms and validating multiplicity, we make everyone different and everyone other.

Norms, however, are not so easily weeded out of our consciousness. We learn them through language which structures consciousness. Language organizes our thought in a particular way. This happens with all the categories we employ to identify ourselves and other people as well. In order to get beyond these categories that see some phenomena as normal and others as strange, pathological, or in need of being fixed, we have to upset the structures of consciousness. One strategy to accomplish that is to play with language. Another is to scrutinize what counts as knowledge and what are the sources of truth. I say more about these in the next two sections.

One of the unique aspects of third wave feminism is its presence in and use of popular culture. Third wave feminists, like many theorists and activists in contemporary times, expand what counts as political and the modes of political activism. Politics is no longer reserved for the formal structures of government or even the more informal relations between people acting together or in opposition in the social sphere. Whereas other waves of feminist theorists hold that political action is collective, third wave feminist theorists valorize individual actions in the marketplace, the academy, and even within one's own mind as political. For some third wave feminists, this means a rejection of collective, group based political action but at other times the individuals are understood to be participating in collective efforts from their individuality. Politics is found in almost every action – the use and creation of popular culture is an important political strategy because of its effects on consciousness.

KNITTING SOCIAL CHANGE

An example of using popular culture for feminist ends is found in 'Stitch and Bitch' clubs based on the knitting books by that name writen by Debbie Stoller. Knitting used to be thought of as something only grandmothers did and while young people and feminists may have known how to knit, they often hid it because they did not want to be stereotyped or participate in such a gendered activity. No more! Now many young knitters not only endorse the activity, they do it socially, in public, and even engage in 'guerilla knitting': knitting for no functional reason, displaying knit objects in public (around telephone poles or parking meters).

The example of knitting (see text box) reveals third wave feminist approaches by showing how one can act in ways that subvert gender expectations while also embracing seemingly gendered norms. By knitting in public one contributes to culture but there is also a challenge to what we understand as 'culture' embedded here. With its functional roots, knitting might not be readily associated with 'culture' but that is precisely the point. Third wave feminism sees the power and possibility of creating culture through formerly disavowed or disparaged crafts. This can be seen also in 'zines' which are privately produced, privately distributed pamphlets on any sort of topic one desires. Blogs, too, exemplify how culture can be created by anyone with a computer. Both zines and blogs illustrate the power of individuals to contribute meaningfully to culture and society. These examples also show how individual people, through small actions, can use popular culture to bring about social change.

Zines, blogs, knitting, indie music, and other third wave activities are self-motivated political activities. So too is selective consumerism. One way to express one's political affiliations or commitments is through how one invests money, what one buys or does not buy, who or what one contributes to, or even the general way one approaches money and economic issues in society. By recognizing politics in every action, third wave feminism has been criticized for emptying politics of content or of neglecting collective action to create social change. This weakness might also be a strength insofar as one can act politically to create social change alone or together and in almost every action one performs insofar as it is performed self-consciously and freely. Of course, critics will nevertheless question the effectiveness of such actions.

The final methodological thread I will mention may seem to contradict some of the previous points but contradiction is not something from which third wave feminists shy. Logic too is criticized as phallocentric by some postmodern feminists. Third wave feminism, like second wave feminism, looks for some way to conceptualize collective action. But much of third wave feminism rejects identity because it is a normalizing concept. Instead, political coalitions may be built across or in spite of ideological differences based on other non-normative factors such as choice or simply the need for a collective political response to a social problem. These coalitions are often very goal oriented and do not last beyond accomplishing the goal. The idea is not to establish a group but rather to bring about social change.

These methodological threads appear in various ways in the topics discussed in the subsequent sections. Importantly, however, feminists do not always agree and do not need to agree. In some sense, to ask that feminists all agree about what they want is itself an oppressive norm that needs to be demolished.

Feminist epistemology and philosophy of science

In the previous chapter, we looked briefly at standpoint episte-mology. Standpoint is one form of feminist epistemology but there are other forms including feminist empiricism, postmod-ern epistemologies, and global feminist epistemologies. Epistemology is the study of knowledge; it is important to feminists because what counts as true and who counts as a knower might be dictated by power relations based on gender, race, class, and other considerations. In a similar way, feminist philosophy of science questions whether bias can enter into the methods of science and into the inquiries explored or accepted by the scientific community.

Feminist epistemology and philosophy of science calls into question the whole notion of objectivity or neutrality in knowl-edge. Some feminist epistemologies remake objectivity to take into account the social position, sex, and race of the knower. Others argue that objectivity is not possible and ought not to be our goal in epistemology. The subjectivity of the knower always enters into the knowledge claims and the study of knowledge.

In traditional science, objectivity is a primary value and the scientific method is designed to maximize objectivity and control for outside influences. Feminists who challenge objec-tivity see the scientific method as useful but limited. It reflects a masculinist view of the world and of the scientist. The scientific method entails the positing of a question, formation of a hypoth-esis, the experiment which includes controls, and conclusions. It also assumes a more or less isolated experimentation and scien-tist. But science is almost always done in a community; feminist philosophers of science tend to shift the focus onto this commu-nity of scholars and away from controlled, reproducible, isolated experiments. What changes is not so much the experiment but rather how we ask questions and interpret the data collected.

Another element of feminist philosophy of science and feminist science studies more generally is the selection of topics for study. This is actually an issue that has played a more prominent role in the popular media – studies of heart disease were historically conducted on men, recommended daily allowances of vitamins took a male body type as the norm, and diseases that solely affected women were often overlooked. Thanks in part to the efforts of feminists in and out of the relevant fields, these sorts of studies are now much more balanced or openly report that findings pertain to only one sex type.

Feminist epistemology overtly claims connections to politics and also reveals the political elements of traditional epistemology. Linda Alcoff succinctly catalogues the connection between politics and epistemology in an article entitled 'How is Epistemology Political?' (1993). Alcoff identifies three relations between politics and epistemology. The first is that epistemology emerges from particular social structures. Those in power set the standards for who counts as an epistemologist and what gets discussed in epistemological contexts. In other words, the powerful in society affirm their social position by rejecting any knowledge claims from people other than themselves. This is certainly evidenced in the relations between genders as well as the relations between colonizer and colonized. The inferior caste contributes folk wisdom or traditional practices but not knowledge. In this way traditional claims of knowledge or reason are sexist and racist. The second relation is one that we have already intimated: that the identity of the theorists themselves is epistemologically relevant. Although she is not applying identity politics, Alcoff does mean that gender privilege affects how one understands – everything from the formulation of hypotheses to the analogies used in explanatory models reflect a person's social location. Finally, the third relation pertains to the effects of knowledge. Scientific and knowledge claims affect society in non-trivial ways and often maintain the position of privilege of the knower.

In addition to the critical elements of feminist epistemology, this approach is used to discuss how people might understand the experience of others who are differently situated. In liberation studies, this is particularly important as it invites the formerly privileged into the liberation struggles with the oppressed but requires that the situation of oppression be understood. A number of feminist epistemologists have questioned the stark binary between reason and emotion in traditional epistemology. To understand the situation of another, we have to reject that binary – emotion is informative and reason without emotion is a remnant of patriarchal epistemologies. As we relate to one another with and through love, we gain a greater understanding of others and their needs.

Truth is not sacrificed in this model but does mean something different than traditional epistemology that values absolute certainty. When we make truth claims we ought also to recognize their rootedness in social and historical locations. We also need to see that truth is limited or conditioned by the language systems that must be used to express it.

Language

The power of language to shape reality – or at least shape how we think about reality – has been noted by theorists from many different disciplines. Feminists are no exception. Language might be overtly sexist, unintentionally patriarchal, or symbolically hegemonic. In response, some liberal and socialist feminists have argued for changes in the public use of language to encourage gender neutrality and non-discrimination, some postmodern feminists have offered *l'écriture feminine* – feminine writing – and new forms of linguistic logic to challenge phallocentrism. And other schools of feminist thought add their own analyses and proposals for challenging sexism in language and thought.

Language that is overtly sexist is fairly easy to recognize but the problem is that some sexist language has been reappropriated for other uses in contexts where the meaning is changed. Take a word like 'pimp.' A pimp is someone who exploits and often abuses women, men, and children by selling them as prostitutes – a practice all feminists would condemn. The word 'pimp,' however, has taken on new meanings in recent years. It is used to describe enhancements to a car and to stand in for something that is 'cool' or 'awesome' (two words that also have multiple slang meanings). Is every use of the word pimp somehow related to sexist exploitation or can there be neutral or tame uses? Other examples of overtly sexist language are the adjectives that are used to describe male and female children. Girls are sweet, nice, quiet, beautiful, and delicate. Boys are strong, tough, serious, and active. Adult women are often described according to their marital status as 'Miss' or 'Mrs' while adult males are referred to solely by 'Mr.' Similarly, the names for male and female professionals sometimes differ, with the female being diminutive of the male as in actress/actor, waitress/waiter, stewardess/steward. Largely due to the efforts of feminist activists, many of these diminutives are dropping out of common usage.

Unintentionally patriarchal language may be found in the use of male pronouns to describe a member of a profession that has traditionally been dominated by men, as in 'A professor always has his scholarship on his mind.' The supposed gender neutrality of using 'he' as the pronoun when the sex of the subject is not known reflects the patriarchal social relations of a particular period in history. Changing the gender dynamics within predominantly male professions includes changing how we refer to those professions. Family names are customarily patronymic – following the father's line – and often reflect a long line of fathers and sons, as in the name 'Johnson' which comes from 'John's son.' Other forms of unintentionally patriarchal language may be found in the grammatical structures of questions posed to women versus those posed to men. For instance, Jean-Jacques Rousseau suggests posing two different sorts of questions to boys and girls regarding moral behavior. Boys are asked about the good of an action while girls are asked about the effect of an action. This may sound rather innocuous but when we also learn that Rousseau values the intentions of moral actions over the consequences, the different questions reveal a perceived inferiority of women.

Postmodern feminists argue that language as a symbolic system is hegemonic, dominant, or phallocentric/phallogocentric. According to Jacques Lacan (1901–1981), society perpetuates itself through the rituals and signs that constitute the 'Symbolic Order.' This Symbolic Order is learned through language. In other words, we learn how to be in society, what roles are appropriate for us, and who we are through language. But Luce Irigaray argues that the Symbolic Order is phallocentric, it is a masculine order and women appear in it as the 'masculine feminine' or as women-the-way-men-understand-women-to-be. Irigaray calls for a liberation from phallocentrism and the Symbolic Order by looking to Lacan's developmental stage prior to the Symbolic Order, the Imaginary. She advocates the creation of a female language that eschews objectivity as a goal and is modeled on feminine sexual pleasure. In her book, *This Sex Which is Not One*, Irigaray uses the metaphor of female sexual pleasure and the multiplicity of female sexual organs to challenge the singularity of phallocentric thought. The title of her book alone reveals something of her project – this is a sex which is not 'one.' Another postmodern feminist, Hélène Cixous, offered a notion of feminine writing or writing women's bodies that employs the logic of multiplicity and fluidity linked to women's embodiment and sexuality. Feminine writing is non-linear and not afraid of contradiction. It rejects, in other words, the masculine hegemonic conception of language and logic.

As we have seen, there are numerous and varied strategies for challenging and changing sexist language. Using gender-neutral language and avoiding sexist language are perhaps the most common tools but some feminist linguists have also addressed the styles or patterns of communication that women use. For instance, women often add a tag question to a declarative statement whereas men tend to state things more authoritatively (as in, woman: 'The economy is very bad today, isn't it?'; and man: 'The economy is bad'). In part this could be due to the same tendency Carol Gilligan noted in the development of the ethics of care. Women might be seeking to develop and maintain relationships while men are asserting their knowledge claims and feigning objectivity. Avoiding that tag question or other forms of hedging might be one way for women to show their assertiveness and power in communication situations. Feminists have already radically transformed language and reality – and we have every reason to believe they will continue to do so in creative and interesting ways.

Sex versus gender debate

Third wave feminism challenges sex and gender constructs, like second wave feminism. But many third wave feminists actually challenge those constructs by embracing them. This is also a rejection of normative notions of gender insofar as any individual may embrace any number of seemingly contradictory gender constructs. So, a woman may be girlish and powerful, or feminine and self-confidently strong. Some third wave feminists defend the use of make-up and plastic surgery for women as a form of self-expression (whereas second wave feminists likely see in both a manifestation of oppressive beauty standards). As you might guess, some find this problematic, especially some feminists who identify as second wave feminists. Third wave feminists defend the practice as a way to empower individual girls and women to freely choose what and who they are.

Another aspect of third wave feminism is gender as performance. Although some of the themes she discusses fall more naturally under the cluster of topics described as second wave in the previous chapter, Judith Butler argues in *Gender Trouble* (1990) that gender performativity – acting out gender in a continual sort of process – actually creates the illusion of stable gender identities. Her work on performativity has been adopted and developed by subsequent theorists within and outside of feminism. Butler criticizes French feminism (like that of Irigaray and Cixous) as essentialist because it relies on a notion of the feminine in articulating feminine writing or the 'feminine feminine.' Gender as performance means that all gender is created artificially through the social practices that define what counts as gender. Butler draws out a vivid example using drag to show that putting on gender is, in a sense, accepting the social norms that define what gender entails.

Some people interpret Butler as denying the category sex altogether and replacing it with gender as performance. But in a later work, *Bodies that Matter* (1993), she challenges that interpretation by arguing that sex – the biological category – is also shaped by material conditioning. In other words, there are no natural males and females just as there are no natural men and women. The bodies that we posit as prior to the discourse that constructs them are a product of discourse.

In a similar way, some third wave feminists argue that desire too is constructed rather than natural. People are not 'naturally heterosexual' or 'naturally homosexual' the argument goes. Sexual identities are rather assumed through their performance, as actions and expressions are made according to cultural norms that define a specific range of desires. By deconstructing natural desire, third wave feminists open the door for malleable desires and what Butler calls 'subversive repetition.' Although bound by the social norms that determine acceptable forms of desire, an individual might try on new forms of desire and subtly begin to unseat the norms. This builds on the discussions of autoeroticism and multiplicity of sexual organs or female pleasure sites of the French postmodern feminists as well as the *Our Bodies, Ourselves* movement (discussed in Chapter 7) of second wave feminism. The emphasis is on empowering or empowered women freely pursuing their own sexual pleasure.

Queer theory

Butler's work has inspired a branch of scholars who reappropriate the name 'queer' from its derogatory slang usage. She has not, however, always accepted or endorsed a connection with queer theory. Queer theory argues for a sort of radical freedom. 'Queering norms' means making all those things that are identifications of what is 'normal' queer – unusual, unexpected, and unpredictable. Everything from self-identity, to behavior, to bodies is subject to performativity and parody. Queer theorists also separate gender and sexuality. Both are variously socially constructed and may transform over time.

Queer theory challenges all sex and gender dichotomies and all identity ascriptions. Not only is the distinction between woman and man meaningless, so are the distinctions between female and male; heterosexual, homosexual, and bisexual; and gay and lesbian. This is a departure from lesbian ethics and other gay rights movements in part because queer theory rejects identity politics. Gay rights advocates traditionally make claims on behalf of an identifiable group. But 'queering the norm' destroys the group – there is no consistent or consistently held identity about which to make claims.

Take, for instance, the issue of transsexual marriage. The mainstream political climate is minimally ambivalent about same-sex marriage in most cultural contexts. But transsexual marriage actually poses an interesting problem. Transsexuals do not identify with the biological sex of their birth and often engage in medical interventions to alter their biological sex. Some also alter only part of their biological sex. If marriage is defined as between one man and one woman, then how do we determine who counts as a man and a woman? If genders and bodies are not rigidly determined by biological sex, or if a trans-sexual decides to only undergo a partial sex change (for example, a woman who wants to be a man but only has the top surgery, keeping the genitals of a female), then determining who is that one man and one woman for the purposes of legal marriage is not so easy.

Queer theory holds that sex comes in many different forms and occurs in many different locations – not just heterosexual genital sex in a private home. Accordingly, sex is not an easy binary biological distinction between male and female, nor is sex itself reducible to hetero- or homosexual intercourse. The sexed body may be intersexual, transsexual, transgendered, old, young, multiracial, rich, poor, and each of these in different ways at different times. No form of sexuality is privileged as 'good sex' while other forms are vilified as 'perverse'; and folks who are not always thought of as having sex, do (elderly, sick, mentally ill, etc.).

Importantly, queer theorists do not limit their subject to sex, gender, and sexuality. Queer theory is used to destabilize all kinds of norms and identities, including race, class, and nation-ality. Norms and identities are a mark of the dominant culture. Liberation, according to queer theory, entails a radical rejection of those identities.

Not surprisingly, some feminists embrace queer theory as an extension of feminism while others think it is actually anti-feminist. When, for instance, a transgendered person adopts traditional conceptions of femininity, then at least some feminists find it problematic rather than liberating. Too simply put, allowing men to be more like 'women' does not seem to be an advantage. Some feminists find the appropriation of queer theory by feminism (and vice versa) androcentric. It relies heavily on the self-determining individual as the experiencing subject. However, at least one important branch within feminism rejects a notion of the individual as self-determining in favor of relational conceptions of the self. Nevertheless, queer theory and feminism agree that rigid gender norms – and most other sorts of norms – are often harmful to the most vulnerable.

Pop culture and images of women

Feminists all over the globe subtly, but consciously, transform the images of women that they perceive to be limiting or oppressive. Popular culture is a primary tool both in distributing negative messages and disseminating liberated or liberating images of women. For instance, activists in Brazil created a soap opera featuring sexually empowered women that has attracted a booming national audience. The soap garnered the attention of sociologists who noticed a decrease in the number of births women had and a change in the divorce rates that these sociologists connect to the portrayal of progressive images of women on the soap opera.

In a much more explicit act of political protest, the Madres de Plaza de Mayo of Argentina donned white head scarves and walked around a public plaza weekly from 1977 to 2006. They were protesting the 'disappearance' of their children in Argentina's Dirty War and beyond. Their protest, like much feminist activism, was explicitly dedicated to peace and justice but by demonstrating they changed social and cultural expecta-tions regarding women's participation in politics. They also offered a new representation of motherhood and challenged the global imagination regarding women's roles. Other women's groups witnessed their example and some have even adopted their methods in order to raise awareness of the effects of war, protest for peace, and continue the struggle for human rights.

African American and Latino American youth often find rather troubling role models in popular culture. Rap and hip hop music is rife with language that dehumanizes, objectifies, violates, and exploits women. Pimping and prostitution, reducing women to body parts, and other degrading actions are often glorified while musicians who live lavish, irresponsible, and violent lifestyles are admired and emulated. Hip hop feminism is one third wave approach to challenging that misogyny. Hip hop feminism looks for avenues to affirm self-worth and value African American culture and Latino American culture within the wider cultural landscape of the United States.

Patricia Hill Collins offers a careful analysis of the sexual myths about Blacks in her book *Black Sexual Politics: African Americans, Gender, and the New Racism* (2005). She shows how the image of white womanhood is built on the sacrifice of women of color as jezebels and other images of women to be discarded. Rap and hip hop music that degrades women as sexual objects not only reflects but reinforces this history of racism and sexism. A crucial part of the process is to recognize the way a history of racism has led to a society full of self-loathing and distrust that is often represented in rap and hip hop music.

The insights regarding internalized or psychological oppression are useful here. As discussed in the last chapter, black or Latino women may internalize the identities found within hip hop culture or others may use these dehumanizing sexualized identities to define and limit them. Fighting back requires changing the message but it also requires unlearning the internalized identities. Hip hop feminism emphasizes the need to address the problem on many fronts. Men need to shake off the oppressive consciousness that keeps them from loving themselves; whites and blacks need to resist the urge to accept the oppressive images of hip hop culture as definitive; and music consumers need to boycott the wealthy record companies and artists who profit from the dehumanization of black and Latina women.

Among the strategies advocated by hip hop feminists and other feminists attuned to the intersections of race and gender is the establishment of a new aesthetic. Echoing the 'Black is Beautiful' movement in the 1960s and 1970s as well as the Harlem Renaissance of the early twentieth century, a new aesthetic finds beauty not in comparison to white, European physical and artistic standards but in accordance with real African American men and women – young and old – who are beautiful and whose artistic accomplishments are admirable. Positive representations of women in hip hop culture are becoming more common and, of course, most black women resist the demeaning images in their own lives. Within Latina feminism, the new aesthetic also takes the form of writing and publishing poetry and prose – claiming one's status as artist.

By using popular culture rather than (or in addition to) more overt forms of feminist argument, activists are often able to transform negative images of women and unhealthy messages about personal relationships or political roles into more open, diverse, and accepting portrayals of women and the many ways women act in society. Hip hop feminism suggests ways that men and women can support each other, and can love each other as 'brothers' and 'sistas.'

Ecofeminism

Combating racism and sexism in culture also involves combating racism and sexism in environmental policies and regulations. 'Environmental racism' denotes the more or less explicitly racist elements of environmental practices. Locating major toxic polluters in close proximity to predominantly black or Latino neighborhoods is a prime example. As a global problem, environmental racism may be seen in everything from the First World's exportation of waste to impoverished nations to the trade agreements that have led to massive outsourcing of manufacturing jobs involving dangerous production methods to countries lacking regulative policies and bodies. One such example that is of particular interest to feminists – and blends racism, sexism, and environmental hazards – are the thousands of maquiladoras in northern Mexico. Maquiladoras are manufacturing factories largely for export goods. Women are recruited to work long hours for little pay in part because of their commitment to stay close to home and because they are perceived to be more docile than male employees. The working conditions are unhealthy with workers and surrounding communities exposed to toxic chemicals or poorly disposed toxic waste. As this example illustrates, issues of race, class, gender, and the environment are often intertwined. Ecofeminism addresses the confluence of oppressive systems with particular emphasis on our connections to the environment and the more-than-human-world.

Ecofeminism might be broadly understood as a blending of ecological concerns with feminist concerns. But this simple description belies a complex body of theory that offers a conception of oppression inclusive of the more-than-human-world and entire ecosystems.

Ecofeminism has ethical, metaphysical, and religious dimensions. There are ecofeminist utopias which envision a world where humans recognize they are part of nature rather than separated from it, and where social relations are non-hierarchical and non-competitive. Some ecofeminists also look to remnants of myths of matriarchal cultures or seek out goddess worship traditions.

Ecofeminism's contribution to moral theory and practice is, among other things, the recognition that humans need to look at the earth differently. Most ecofeminists base their ethic on some theory from the ecology movement. For example, some feminists might appeal to 'deep ecology,' which asserts the intrinsic value of every life-form. Others might look to 'social ecology,' which distinguishes between a biological 'first nature' and a human social 'second nature,' for the basis of their ecofeminist ethics. Still others argue that the entire earth is alive; they challenge mechanistic or instrumental understandings of humankind's relationship with the world and replace it with a view of human interconnectedness with non-human nature. For ecofeminists or feminists concerned with the natural world, humans are part of an interconnected web of life and not necessarily the center of that web.

Other ecofeminist philosophies – in addition to the ethics – offer non-dualistic conceptions of metaphysics. By rejecting the nature/human dichotomy, they encourage a fresh, new examination of human identity, politics, and religion. Moreover, the domination of nature often adversely affects women and the poor first. Ecofeminists challenge the ecology movement to see how gender, race, and class also ought to be the focus of environmental concerns.

This is what makes this theory 'feminist' and not merely ecology: it draws parallels between human domination of the earth and males' domination of females. Indeed, a quick look at how the earth is often described offers clues to these parallels. For instance, we speak of 'Mother Earth' and 'Mother Nature,' and when great destruction is perpetrated by humans on this 'Mother' we call it 'the rape of nature.' The parallel between these two systems of domination reveals that addressing singular manifestations of domination, as some branches of the woman's movement and the ecology movement have done, is insufficient. Instead, our thinking and ethical obligations must be expanded to include a confrontation of all systems of domination and hierarchy. The goal is to achieve a life-affirming, sustainable existence without systems of domination.

By way of example, animal rights ecofeminists might adopt a vegetarian or vegan lifestyle. Vegans do not eat or use animal products. Vegetarians offer moral justifications for their position, and those justifications range from the animal's right not to be harmed by humans to the social distribution of resources. It takes sixteen pounds of grain to produce one pound of beef and the richest countries consume more than their fair share of the grain and meat. Ecofeminists take a different approach. An ecofeminist justification for a vegetarian lifestyle might include some of these other justifications for vegetarianism but it would also likely utilize some feminist analysis as well. Many ecofeminist vegans argue that consuming milk and eggs participates in the exploitation of the feminine. Milk and eggs, after all, come from females and if environmental concerns are tied up with feminist concerns, then some attention to that fact is called for.

Ecofeminism has been criticized by other feminists as well as non-feminists for (1) drawing what appear to be rather speculative conclusions about matriarchal goddess societies; (2) lacking credibility in positing the intrinsic value of inanimate objects and the earth; and (3) joining ecology and feminism in a way that at times seems to assert women's moral superiority or excluding men from ecological or environmental concern. While simultaneously blaming men for the mechanistic, instrumental abuse of the environment, some ecofeminism appears to eschew men's participation in the revaluing of the earth and its resources.

In spite of these criticisms, in the current age of global climate change concomitant with the recognition that we humans are at least partially responsible, the insights of ecofeminism seem particularly relevant. Ecofeminists have always argued for the interconnections between humans and the more-than-human-world. We are now feeling some of the negative repercussions of failing to appreciate that fact.

Disability and feminism

Another important insight in contemporary third wave feminism is found in the intersection between disability studies and feminist theory. Like feminism, disability studies challenges the 'normative' conceptions of the body: ideas that hold there is a normal body. When conceptions of a normal body dominate the public imagination, then deviations from that norm are considered disabilities – an individual is disabled. But recent work in disability studies questions that assumption. Instead, disability is a result of social structures that make it more difficult for some bodies to function than other bodies. For example, consider visual impairment versus motility. The normative conception of vision is quite wide and society (here represented by signage, insurance companies, social standards of beauty, etc.) makes allowances for imperfect vision. For the most part, unless a visual impairment is severe, an individual is able to function like those people who do not have a 'vision problem.' It is, in other words, a socially accepted 'disability.' But not all disabilities are accommodated so readily. Motility is a good counter example. If a person's ability to move and get around in society is impaired because of a body that is different from the bodies of most people, or at least the people in power, then that person may not be able to function in the same way as others who do not have this different body.

Feminists who work on the intersections between disability and feminism argue that by pathologizing the non-normative body we misconstrue disability. They argue that disability is a failure of the social system not a flaw in a given body. The social system perpetuates a hierarchy of bodies that approximate the norm and often fails to invest in the structural changes that would allow those bodies furthest from the norm to function well and contribute meaningfully to the social whole. When university and government building entrances are only available via stairs, people who use wheel chairs are effectively barred from admittance. When communication or conversation occurs over a phone line a person who is deaf is excluded from the communication, information, or conversation. The United Nations Convention on the Rights of Persons with Disabilities, adopted in December 2006 (preceded by the Declaration of the Rights of Disabled Persons in 1975), made great strides in changing the social perception of disability. Rather than treating people with disabilities as objects requiring assistance, the UN Convention emphasizes the rights and subjectivity of individuals with disabilities. By shifting thinking about disability away from an individual with a physical problem to a society with an accommodation problem, the Convention stresses the social obligation to provide accessible buildings, phone lines equipped with technology for the hearing impaired, and numerous other changes to ensure the full participation of people with disabilities in society. The Charter of Fundamental Rights of the European Union (Article 26 Integration of Persons with Disabilities) and domestic policies within nation-states similarly support a shift in thinking about disability. Feminists contribute to this analysis by applying some of the insights from feminist ethics, epistemology, and other theories to disability studies and also borrowing or learning from disability studies for new ways to think about feminism.

Feminist ethics of care is used by many feminist theorists to articulate some of the issues the disabled and their caregivers confront interpersonally, in the medical establishment, and in society more broadly. Feminist bioethics – sometimes based in an ethics of care and sometimes based in other feminist ethical models – similarly raises and analyzes issues pertaining to the disabled. What makes these issues feminist is both the methods used and the content of the issues. The methods draw on non-hierarchical ethical considerations, involve a relational conception of the self, and frequently use personal narrative to draw out ethical claims. Among the many feminist issues are relations between caregivers and the cared for, sexuality and disability, rights to bear and rear children, and rape and abuse of the disabled.

Feminist epistemology is useful in helping communicate the needs and desires of differently situated peoples. Recall that one feminist epistemological proposal involved trying to see the world through the imagination of the other. Often when a person confronts a disability in another person, the tendency is to imagine what it would be like to be that other person and extrapolate from one's own experience. For instance, if an able-bodied person sees someone without the use of her arm, that able-bodied person might remember what it was like living with a sprained wrist and imagine the other's disability through that limited experience. The proposal from feminist epistemology, however, is to imagine her disability through her experience. This involves lovingly listening and learning from the person in an effort to understand the place of disability in her life and truly the place of her disability in one's own life. How does your interpretation of her disability affect her experience? Does she sense a pitying gaze from an able-bodied person? Does she feel reduced to her unusable arm? These questions – and many more – beg to be answered if anything like an adequate understanding of disability is possible. Of course, feminism is not alone in exploring how one can better understand the experience of others – similar insights might be found in oppression studies more generally and in moral theory as well.

The intersection of disability studies and feminism is also fruitful in thinking about how transgendered people have been treated in the past and what sorts of alternatives might be envisioned. If disability is something wrong with society rather than something wrong or lacking in the individual, then rather than trying to 'fix' the transgendered person by making them conform to one of only two gender possibilities that also accords with a presumed biological sex, we might instead try to fix the social expectations and norms that assume gender and sex fall along such easy binaries. We might think in terms of multiple genders and multiple sexes without needing to label or reduce people to only one. And, of course, a person may decide to be multiple genders throughout the course of life. Effecting this sort of radical change is no easy task – we would have to give up on our gendered pronouns for starters. But language is very fluid and responds to social movements quite rapidly.

Youth culture and poor women

Second wave feminists proudly claimed the name 'feminist' but not all third wave feminists elect to call themselves feminists or even see themselves as part of the feminist movement. Instead, many young women adopt what they call 'girl culture' or 'youth culture.' They see the power in being a girl – not in using sexual appeal but rather the personal power to be strong and do whatever you want. Some proudly wear pink, hair-bows and knee-socks, carry purses meant for very young girls, and otherwise brandish their personal style. While one might be tempted to say such actions are infantilizing or perhaps even complicit in the oppression of women, youth culture feminists see it as self-determination and pride in one's personal power.

Grrl power celebrates the power of youth culture and self-consciously assumes a name that some feminists would call demeaning or infantilizing. The double r of Grrl also indicates anger and aggression. Grrl power is a movement to claim agency and effectiveness in spite of a culture that devalues contributions from young people. Third wave feminism works to bring girls and women to feminism by breaking feminism out of the ranks of upper and middle class educated women. Youth, poor women, women from rural areas, and many other women and groups previously marginalized from the workings of feminist theory and the ranks of feminist activists all contribute to feminism in the third wave.

Youth culture and grrl power actually exist, of course, because of feminist gains. Many young men and women in the United States and Europe today believe that women are equal – not just that women are perceived as equal or are equal under the law. With that as their starting point, many third wave feminists are confident that they can embrace any personal identity – feminine or not – and make themselves into whatever they wish. But women are not actually treated equally all over the world or even in the US and Europe.

A sort of flip-side to the youth culture feminism is the sexualization of younger and younger girls. On the one hand, this may be indicative of a cultural acceptance of women claiming their right to sexual pleasure. But on the other hand, it could be a backlash against feminist gains by sexually objectifying very young children. Some feminists will see empowerment and grrl power in the sexually provocative fashions for preteen girls while others will vilify the sexist fashion industrial complex.

Some feminists both in and out of this third wave youth culture have argued that third wave feminism lacks a clear political agenda and third wave feminists lack political consciousness. We have already seen one of the counter arguments – that third wave feminism uses such things as cultural production and conscious consumerism as a political tool. Even if young girls from relatively affluent backgrounds feel that they are not oppressed and hence feel alienated from other feminist agendas, there are still social justice causes – many of which pertain to their own lives as females or as sexual beings – that are worthy of coalitional politics to bring about social change.

Finally, feminist theory has long been the purview of college educated women and women working in academia. That has not, however, been the location for much feminist activism, even if some of this activism and other acts of resistance are not always recognized as feminist. Academic feminist theory is criticized for failing to acknowledge the contributions from differently situated women – not just the young but also the poor and disenfranchised. Poor women have always been involved in action and resistance but theory building has also always had a classist slant – 'theorists' are only those with the leisure time to think and write. Deconstructing that myth opens up new insights and new strategies for feminism. The next chapter addresses a similar concern on the global scale.

6

Postcolonial, transnational, and global feminisms

Just as business, technology, communication, and politics have become more globalized, so has feminist theory. This globalization offers many challenges and promises for feminist theory. The meeting of cultures is always informative even if it is also sometimes combative. As globalization of feminism takes root, feminists must try to reconcile the efforts to work on behalf of all women with the respect and appreciation of cultural differences. Often that reconciliation is particularly problematic because of deeply ingrained beliefs and practices about women and women's place in some societies. Feminists have to be careful when criticizing societies other than their own and yet that is one of the tasks of global feminism. Importantly, though, criticism alone is never enough. Global feminism strives to build connections between women around the world based on collective political commitments to social change.

Susan Moller Okin once suggested that just as academic feminists and academic feminist theory turned toward an emphasis on the differences between women, as we saw with third wave feminism, women's activists all over the world sought connections between women. These activists found in the commonalities among women and the similarities in forms of oppression some basis for coalitional politics to argue for the human rights of all women. Global feminists acknowledge the class, cultural, religious, and ethnic differences among women but nevertheless find common ground for political action. This is coalitional politics.

As Okin further argued, women all over the world need support from Western feminists and from the international community generally. A global feminism must be able to both find reasons for collective action to ensure the human rights of women while also criticizing those cultural practices, even within one's own culture, that are harmful to women. But, importantly, global feminism and transnational feminism explode the usual trajectory of aid – they caution against models or theories that posit the 'two-thirds world' as being in need of assistance from the 'one-third world'. Such models fail to recognize the agency and power of women and men in the developing world. Those terms – 'two-thirds world' and 'one-third world' – vividly illustrate the relation between those who 'have' and those who 'have not.' A minority of the people in the world live in industrialized countries. Most people, two-thirds of the world, live in the Global South, Third World, or lesser developed countries. These terms are controversial however. One can live in 'third-world conditions' amidst first world splendor. Additionally, referring to industrialization as 'developed' indicates a singularly Western model of progress. For these reasons, the transnational and global feminists and other activists for more equitable distribution of the world's resources sometimes employ the one-third/two-third terminology or use the other terminology with political consciousness and perhaps even infuse new meaning in old concepts, like 'Third World.'

Building bridges between feminist groups and other women's groups is a political act that does not require shared experience or common identity. Key concepts in global feminist theory are human rights, coalition or solidarity, and empowerment. Human rights are the basic rights of every human and usually include both positive and negative rights. Positive rights are rights to something, like the right to leisure time, the right to a decent job, the right to a just wage and safe working conditions. Negative rights are protections, such as the right not to have one's property unjustly or arbitrarily taken by the state, the right to practice one's religion free from interference so long as doing so does not infringe on the basic rights of others, and the right not to be tortured.

Solidarity is a unity of people around a common goal. It entails commitments to that goal as well as to others who are similarly committed. In an analogous way, coalitions are connections between and among people or groups for political ends. Global feminists use these concepts to demonstrate the connections among women's groups across national borders and despite linguistic differences. They indicate the positive power that comes from working together for a common end perhaps even in spite of deep ideological differences.

Empowerment in feminist theory generally means the power an individual or group recognizes in itself. This is a power to transform the self or group and often extends to transforming the lives of others, social structures, and society in general. Often, when people are victimized by oppression, they fail to see their own power. The process of liberation then is also a process of empowerment – a freeing from the bonds that keep one from seeing and acting on or with one's own power.

Global feminism looks at issues that affect women globally or from a global perspective. That is, there are some issues that seem to affect women all around the world such as sex and gender based harassment and violence. Other issues require a global perspective with a feminist consciousness, such as consumerism. Buying and selling products is a political action, as third wave feminists argue. Global feminists make that political project global by considering the effects of purchases on women and children around the globe. As I mentioned above, one of the central elements to global feminism is human rights. The

United Nations Universal Declaration of Human Rights (1948) is the most sweeping and widely accepted account of human rights but in practice it is far from universal. Global feminists' interest in this document is multifaceted. They point out that many cultures still fail to acknowledge women as fully human, much less as legal persons worthy of rights protections. The document itself makes scant reference to gender and does not cover sex specific violations of human rights at all. Global feminists offer specific strategies to extend human rights to women, including obtaining full legal status for women, and modifying current human rights standards to account for sex and gender specific violations.

The term 'global feminism' is often used interchangeably with 'transnational feminism.' Nevertheless, there is a discernible difference between the two. Transnational feminism transcends national borders. It need not, however, engage global concerns though it might do this also. An example of transnational feminism is when women in a developed country work with women in a less developed country to create opportunities for women, and trade information and knowledge.

For instance, Norwegian women's groups have worked with women's groups in Thailand to try to stem the tide of human trafficking from Thailand to Norway. Among the ways they do this is through funding grants for women's centers at universities, offering loans for women's co-operatives to help support and sustain alternative sources of income, and funding the establishment of programs to educate people about the true intent of the recruiters who come to villages seeking domestic workers for the city. But transnational feminism cannot be a unidirectional effort. The women's groups of Thailand also must work to educate the women's groups in Norway. They must explain their cultural traditions and practices that make some women more vulnerable to trafficking than others and describe what sorts of alternatives will make a difference in the lives of poor women. Moreover, whether from the universities or the villages, the women of Thailand also challenge the women of Norway to address the problem of human trafficking by targeting the traffickers and the consumers, johns, or others who book sex vacations to Thailand or send for mail order brides from Southeast Asia. In other words, the challenge to Norway is to examine the causes of trafficking from the demand side.

What we see from this example is an emphasis on how women can work together in the struggle for human rights and women's rights in spite of national borders. Cultural practices, linguistic barriers, and governmental policies often hamper the ability of women's groups to work together, however. Global and transnational feminisms aim to respect cultures and national sovereignty while they also challenge sexist elements of both. This is not always an easy line to walk. Often, one has to confront the problems in one's own country first in order to even be trusted by women's groups in another country. If the policies of the United States directly and adversely impact the women of El Salvador, for instance, then before women's groups in the US are able to fully participate with equality with women in El Salvador to bring about social change, they need to change the US government policy. Trust is part of what is at stake but so is courage and honesty. Just as on the personal level one must confront one's own sexism before criticizing the sexism of others, so too must one confront those things that contribute to sexist discrimination or violence in one's country before or while criticizing others.

Other approaches to feminism that cross borders or span the globe in their concerns and adherents are postcolonial feminism and Third World feminism. These share many commonalities with global feminism and transnational feminism insofar as they pay attention to the concerns and diversity of race, class, culture, nationality, ethnicity, and religion as well as sex. In that sense, these forms of feminism are often grouped together or referred to similarly. But postcolonial feminism and Third World feminism do have some unique theoretical characteristics as well.

Postcolonial feminism traces many of the problems of less developed countries back to the histories of colonialism. Colonialism exploited not just natural resources; it also hijacked cultures, educational systems, beliefs about race and gender relations, and languages. Postcolonial feminism analyzes sexist ideologies and practices within this context. Postcolonial feminists are a widely diverse group. They may reside either in the former colonies or in Europe or America. They might be descended from the colonizers or the colonized. Regardless, their analytical framework is the history of colonialism and its enduring effects.

Of course, not every colony experienced colonialism in the same way. Imperialist regimes treated the peoples within the nations they colonized quite differently. This diversity of experience is important in thinking about postcolonial feminism as well. Many postcolonial feminists see remnants of colonialism in the universalizing claims of other feminists. When first and second wave feminists, for instance, argued from the basis of oppression in women's shared experience, they overlooked or ignored the numerous ways that women did not and do not share similar experiences. Postcolonial feminists highlight the ways some feminist schools of thought and projects repeat dominant relations or reinscribe oppressive identities. When feminists impose Western models of liberation on the two-thirds world, they engage in a sort of neocolonialism that echoes the historical experience of colonialism by trying to make the 'colony' more like them.

Although colonialism in the form of political appropriation of territory is for the most part a thing of the past, a new form of colonialism is targeted by postcolonial thinkers. Multinational corporations and global businesses, largely centered in Western nations, bring their own colonizing influence through business models, hegemonic culture, exploitation of workers, and displacement of traditional trades. Whereas traditional forms of colonialism entailed the colonizer assuming the privilege of ruling in the colony, this neocolonialism rules indirectly through the power it creates and enjoys by bringing manufacturing jobs to an area or providing consumer goods to a people – often Western inspired consumer goods as well. Old style colonialism often killed or displaced indigenous peoples; the new style of colonialism impoverishes a culture by swamping societies with Western values, products, or ideals.

Colonialism of both sorts becomes an obvious feminist issue when sexist oppression is present but postcolonial feminists also argue that there are important connections between sexism and racism, colonialism, classism, heterosexism, ecological injustice, and other forms of oppression. Although postcolonial feminist strategies for liberation require acknowledging differences among peoples and experiences, the analyses of oppression might be broadly understood under the same umbrella structure. They emphasize that the history of colonization and oppression is fundamental to the identity and experience of oppressed peoples, and that often multiple forms of oppression simultaneously intersect to affect social existence.

In a similar vein, Third World feminists challenge racism, sexism, colonialism, and imperialism by emphasizing strength and resistance in the face of hegemonic culture. Although residing in both wealthy nations and poorer nations, Third World feminists describe their locations as 'Third World' to indicate the conditions of poverty, exploitation, and marginalization that may be experienced wherever one resides. The name 'Third World' itself issues from a colonial past but has been appropriated by feminists and other activists in order to describe the political unity against oppression. One key element to this resistance is the rejection of the colonial histories written from the perspective of the imperialist colonizer. Instead, Third World feminists advocate rewriting history from the perspective and experience of colonized peoples. This adds particularity to history and avoids the totalizing claims of former imperialists. In addition, Third World feminists use the specific efforts of survival in the day to day lives of colonized and formerly colonized peoples to guide theory.

Both postcolonial feminists and Third World feminists argue that the solution to the oppression of women is for individuals and peoples to have the liberty to shape their own destinies in light of their oppressed histories. In order to do this, they need freedom from dominant cultures as well as imperialist nations. Daily, humans form communities of resistance that unite them in struggles for human dignity and against oppressive forces. As every human rights activist will assert, human dignity requires economic and political self-determination. Breaking free from the imperialist forces of dominant culture is crucial to those struggles.

One concrete strategy of resistance – in addition to those practiced in day to day efforts to survive and more overt efforts for social and political change – is writing. Feminists of all kinds have used personal narrative, or writing one's story, as a way to discover one's own subjectivity and assert agency in opposition to oppressive forces. Third World and postcolonial feminists use writing to claim the memories of valued cultural traditions, colonized and violent histories, and family honor.

Global, transnational, postcolonial, and Third World feminists address numerous issues in their efforts to advance women's rights and challenge sexist or patriarchal structures globally. An important element of global feminist theory is to examine issues as interconnected and mutually reinforcing. Addressing feminization of poverty, for instance, must take into account issues of race and class domestically and internationally while also confronting the gendered aspects of poverty.

Similarly, other issues, such as human trafficking or rape in conflict situations, may contribute to the feminization of poverty and vice versa. The next few sections present some of these issues and illustrate the complex analysis necessary for women's liberation worldwide.

> **THE UNITED NATIONS FOURTH WORLD CONFERENCE ON WOMEN BEIJING PLATFORM FOR ACTION, PARAGRAPH 17**
>
> 'Absolute poverty and the feminization of poverty, unemployment, the increasing fragility of the environment, continued violence against women and the widespread exclusion of half of humanity from institutions of power and governance underscore the need to continue the search for development, peace and security and for ways of assuring people-centred sustainable development. The participation and leadership of the half of humanity that is female is essential to the success of that search. Therefore, only a new era of international cooperation among Governments and peoples based on a spirit of partnership, an equitable, international social and economic environment, and a radical transformation of the relationship between women and men to one of full and equal partnership will enable the world to meet the challenges of the twenty-first century.'

Feminization of poverty

Of the people in poverty worldwide, over two-thirds are female. This fact alone should make us pause to ask how poverty is a gender issue. Industrialized nations often have a history of pay disparity between men and women that may contribute to more women ending up in poverty. If a woman's wage is significantly lower than a man's and if she is a single parent, then her ability to provide for herself and her children is vastly different than a man in a similar situation. In less developed nations, women's social status may contribute to lower economic status. Sociologists and economists also provide convincing data that indicate that women are more likely to sacrifice their own well-being for their families than are men. This observation becomes very important when considering the distribution of aid to needy families. If men are more likely to take aid and spend it on themselves rather than their families, or, to put it another way, if women are more likely to use aid to benefit their families, then development assistance should be targeted toward women and female heads of households. The problem is that often there are deeply entrenched gender biases against women as financial managers of households.

The 'feminization of poverty,' a term introduced in the late 1970s by Diana Pearce, marks these changes. As the concept implies, poverty has become more 'feminized.' Among other things, that means that the majority of people in poverty are women, the gap between the number of men in poverty and the number of women in poverty has increased, more female-headed households already in poverty are finding it hard to get out of that situation, and the effects of poverty affect women and children more than men. The feminization of poverty invites a new approach to thinking about poverty issues. In addition to looking at the causes and consequences of poverty, the concept demands a look into the types and causes of social inequalities based on gender.

Gender biases, unequal wages, and familial burdens make it more difficult for women to come out of poverty. Other factors include the gender gap in education and healthcare. If women receive substandard education, lack training or opportunity for advancement, and also have increased responsibilities in the domestic sphere, then they are less likely to be able to obtain good jobs with sustainable wages. Moreover, women may be prohibited from even applying for some jobs because of culturally sanctioned gender discrimination. In some poor regions of the world, there may also be additional factors. Girls may be excluded from education so that the male children of a family may attend school. Girls may be given – or even sold – into various forms of indentured servitude or slavery and be unable to escape for fear of their safety or the safety of their families. The exploitation of girls and women all over the world certainly contributes to the feminization of poverty.

Additional factors that may make it harder for women to get out of poverty are legal and cultural barriers that keep women from owning property, for example, when inheritance is passed to the oldest living male relative. A woman whose husband dies may find herself at the mercy of a brother-in-law, nephew, or even her own son. Social services, social security, or welfare, in some cultures, are not as widely distributed to women as they are to men. Healthcare too might pose an almost insurmountable obstacle to a woman's ability to escape poverty. For instance, state funded healthcare may not always provide for gender specific needs or medical assistance may not have the resources to provide for the specific requirements of women's health. An example might be the cost and availability of birth control for poor women. Even when some basic healthcare is provided by the state or a charitable organization, a woman in poverty may find provisions for basic hygiene more difficult to come by.

Recognizing the gender dimensions of poverty is an important step to bringing about change. Global feminists from a wide variety of schools of thought and cultural traditions have suggested proposals for ameliorating poverty for women. The UN Fourth World Congress on Women, held in 1995 in Beijing, offers one of the clearest examples of coalitional politics to address an issue. Women and women's groups from all over the world came together to address what they perceived as the most pressing issues confronting women. Violence against women was the most dominant then but the feminization of poverty also received attention. That meeting issued a document called the 'Beijing Platform for Action' that calls on the international community to make significant changes to address many of the problems women face worldwide. On the issue of poverty, the Platform for Action recommended legal measures to ensure gender equality, macro- and microeconomic reforms that address the many ways women and children experience poverty, peace and security to help stabilize economic systems, and recognition of the paid and unpaid contributions women make to the economy. Although not specifically recommended, micro-credit or micro-lending has been very successful in Bangladesh and gained international attention when Muhammad Yunus, founder of the Grameen Bank, won the Nobel Peace Prize in 2006. Micro-lending provides small community loans to help women start businesses. With a relatively small amount of money, many women have been able to pull themselves, their families, and their communities out of poverty. While these and other proposals from the Platform for Action specifically and global feminists more generally have brought about some tremendous gains for women, the reality described by the concept 'feminization of poverty' continues.

Global care chains

In Chapter 4 we discussed how feminists had transformed ethics through the ethics of care. Global feminists take it a step further by scrutinizing global care chains. A global care chain is a chain of caregivers connected through contractual relations. When a wealthy First World woman hires a poor woman from another country to come to her home to care for her children, a care chain is formed. But the chain might extend even further. The poorer woman may have left her own children back in her home country. In that case, she may hire another woman (for even lower wages) to care for her children or she may rely on family members to take over her domestic and familial duties. So while a woman in the West enjoys her relative freedom with the help of a domestic servant from a Third World country – and the domestic servant is able to make more money than she would in her own country – the Third World domestic worker has had to give up something important: her motherly relation with her own children.

One aspect of this relationship is the contractual agreement between caregivers for a transfer of caring services from one person to another. At times this is spelled out quite thoroughly in a service contract. At other times, it is an agreement based on a handshake. Moreover, caring is generally not a nine-to-five job and some hours are much more work intensive than others. If an employment contract does not specify the hours as well as the wages, then the hired caregiver risks being exploited. In addition, with or without a clear contract, employers and caregivers alike may attempt to foster a friendly (caring) relationship between each other. While such a relationship may prove fruitful insofar as it opens the way for an exchange of culture, it may also be exploited if the employer expects certain things from a friend that would not be expected from an employee. For instance, when employers invoke ties of friendship to ask caregivers to be available at the last minute or during scheduled off-duty times, the employee is being exploited. The domestic worker and employer are never equal in the relationship and to feign friendship, which itself is rooted in equality, merely disadvantages the worker. The employer has power over the worker in terms of the wage that is paid and may also have power over the worker in terms of the worker's immigration status, linguistic barriers, distance from home country, cultural and familial isolation, and overall vulnerability.

Another element of global care chains is the care. Caregivers often develop deep love relationships with those for whom they care. But when a caregiver has left her own children in her home country, she is not also able to demonstrate her love for her own children on a daily basis. This is not to say that she no longer loves them or that the child for whom she cares is more important than her own children (although both of those might be the case in any given situation). The point is rather that it becomes much more difficult to demonstrate care for one's own children when they are separated by national borders, oceans, or continents. This fact may make us rethink what counts as care or it may make us criticize global care chains for the way they deprive some poor children of the love of their mothers so that wealthy women can work outside the home or enjoy more leisure, free of domestic responsibilities.

A third point about global care chains is that they often rely on or reinforce gender divisions of labor. Even the interactions between the wealthy employers may rely on gender divisions of labor. Frequently, the wealthy family who seeks to hire a domestic worker or live-in caregiver relegates the hiring and management of that domestic worker to the woman, seeks only female applicants, and expects traditionally feminine modes of interaction with all family members (quiet, nurturing, and attentive, but also deferential, submissive, and passive). Any problems that subsequently ensue would also typically be the responsibility of the female – her failure to hire an adequate caregiver for 'her' children, her inability to be a 'proper mother' herself, or simply the gendered expectations that all things that pertain to children fall to the woman.

Caregivers usually leave their home country for the promise of better wages, exposure to or adventure in a new culture, or perhaps because they have been sold into servitude by their family members. In some circumstances, the female caregiver is already a trained professional with a college degree. Employers are attracted to such caregivers for obvious reasons but also because of what Joan Tronto calls 'competitive mothering.'

Essentially, employers who hire a caregiver skilled in some other profession or armed with a college education also get the benefit of those skills in the education and early training of their children while only paying for the care.

Finally, global care chains are global. They unite women across borders but that unity is not always desirable. While global care chains might contribute to a generation of youth (wealthy youth) growing up with an awareness of a culture and language other than their own thanks to the domestic caregiver hired by their parents, that awareness comes at a price. Not only will these young people grow up understanding that they can hire others to do dirty work (including cleaning up dirty diapers and vomit) and nurturing work for them, but they might also believe that other women's children are not as important as their mother's children.

Human trafficking

The 'global market' usually describes legal trade between nations but there is another form of trade that infects the global market – the illegal trade in human beings. This trade, mentioned in my discussion of the feminization of poverty, is called 'human trafficking' and primarily affects women and children. Women and girls are recruited on the promise of a large payoff, sold into servitude by parents or guardians, or stolen from their homes. Women are targeted for trafficking so that they may be used for prostitution, mail order brides, or domestic slavery. Children are targeted for these same purposes but also for illegal adoption and child soldiers. Humans might also be trafficked for the harvesting of their organs.

Postcolonial feminists argue that human trafficking is a form of neocolonialism or an extension of colonialist pasts. Whereas the colonialism that marked so much of European history from the fifteenth to the twentieth centuries exploited the natural resources of the colonies, human trafficking exploits the human resources of these now former colonies.

Global feminists analyze the causes of human trafficking and the 'sexploitation' of women and offer a variety of proposals to protect women and girls and prevent their being trafficked. In addition, they offer specific recommendations for the prosecution of traffickers as well as the rehabilitation and reintegration of women into a non-exploitative society.

In order to prevent human trafficking, global feminists argue that, in addition to the practical steps of providing alternative sources of income for women and legal prosecution of traffickers, there must be: (1) explicit condemnation of human trafficking as a human rights violation by the United Nations and other regional and international governing bodies; (2) social and cultural transformations that value women in themselves and not as bodies for consumption or commodities to be traded and sold; (3) a broadened conception of liberation that recognizes that the liberation of everyone is bound up together. When some human beings are used as objects for the pleasure of others, all human beings are degraded.

The first of these steps is well underway. The United Nations and the European Union both have specific provisions against trafficking in persons as well as offices and dedicated personnel to address the problem. Nevertheless, disreputable travel agents continue to book 'sex vacations' and advertise that a person can have sex with a virgin or an underage girl. Travel brochures even advertise that clients can do things that are illegal in their own countries. A social and cultural transformation that values all women in themselves is slower in coming. Even among those countries whose women appear most liberated, there is still enough of a system of domination or oppression that some women – especially poor women – remain vulnerable. Different schools of feminist thought would, of course, propose different strategies for changing the ideology of domination and bringing about a more equitable condition for women. Marxist and socialist feminists might highlight the need for adequate paying jobs and other social system reforms that keep women from falling into poverty – and avoid gross disparities in the distribution of wealth. Liberal feminists might argue that the legal measures set up to prevent trafficking and prosecute the traffickers are themselves enough to bring about social transformation in how we think about women. And some radical feminists might even suggest that properly used extreme forms of punishment – like castration – for the traffickers would not only have a deterrent effect for other would-be traffickers but it would also have significant symbolic meaning.

Feminists have always thought of liberation as more than just an individualistic pursuit. It is not enough that only some women are able to 'succeed.' Human trafficking further emphasizes the need to expand the concept of liberation. Race, class, and gender oppression all converge in the problem of human trafficking. But in addition, when other human beings are bought and sold for their sexual services, bodies, or body parts, then all humans are degraded. We become mere objects; insofar as we treat others as objects, we subject ourselves to the same fate. Moreover, the prevalence of trafficking means that we are all culpable in some way. While we may not directly partake in the activities of trafficking, when we fail to prevent the commodification of others, we implicitly condone it. Some radical feminists might also add that such things as pornography and prostitution, and perhaps even the use of women as sex objects in advertising, are milder forms of human trafficking. If they are right about that, then trafficking is a problem in every community.

The recognition of our interconnections can lead to coalitional politics as women and men from very different social locations and backgrounds fight the problem from different angles. Mothers in Thailand may find ways to resist the recruiters who come to their homes. Professional women and men in Thailand may work to educate those girls and families who are most vulnerable to the recruiters. Young and old women may pool their resources and talents to create a weaving co-operative that could provide the economic security that would keep families from facing a choice about selling a daughter into servitude. Women in other countries might contribute by aggressively pursuing government policies to prosecute traffickers. Other women from other nations might contribute in similar ways – providing start-up funding for the co-ops, studying the effects of small business on the recruitment capabilities of traffickers, scrutinizing their national ideologies to uncover implicit ways those ideologies condone sexploitation and sexism. Although some co-operation among all these efforts lends to their strength, co-operation and co-ordination is not always possible or desirable. The last section of this chapter examines some of the prospects and problems for coalitional politics or global feminist political solidarity.

An additional concern with human trafficking is how to rehabilitate the children and adults if and when they are rescued from the slavery of human trafficking. Reintegrating them into their home communities is often quite difficult. Here again, cultural standards pose significant obstacles. When recruiters come to a village in Thailand, for instance, they target the village because of its poverty. With the promise of steady work with a high wage doing domestic work, they lure girls away. But it is not always or even usually the girls themselves who are duped – and sometimes it isn't even a matter of deception. Parents and guardians will sometimes knowingly sell their daughters or female charges into indentured servitude or sex slavery. If a girl escapes and returns to her village, these guardians may even return her to the recruiter or trafficker. Although I have used Thailand as my example, it is important to note that women are trafficked from almost every nation, including wealthy Western countries. Some cultures will ostracize or even kill a woman who returns to her community because she is no longer pure.

In order for rehabilitation and reintegration into the community to take place, whole communities have to be transformed. The transformation entails social and economic changes to keep recruiters at bay as well as ideological changes that may radically alter the relationships between men and women, parents and children.

Second wave feminists popularized the expression 'the personal is political.' Global feminists embrace the expression trumpeted by so many activists: 'think globally, act locally.' Combating human trafficking exemplifies this expression in action. Theorists and activists have to see how their local practices impact the global environment for women. By thinking globally, feminists are forced to recognize the women's rights issues beyond their parochial concerns. In this way, too, we can see that global feminism is a critical project. It is critical not just of social systems and global institutions that harm women but of traditional Western feminisms that fail to see the day to day struggles of women around the world as central to feminist theory and practice.

War rape

International law has always had a focus on conflict situations between nations but only recently has the violence against women during conflict situations been addressed. In spite of the fact that the father of international law, Hugo Grotius, actually includes a caution against rape in his discussion of war, women have long been thought of as part of the spoils of war. In many parts of the world, that view still holds sway. But even when women are not considered mere property to be exchanged between vanquished and victor, frequently they are subject to unjustifiable attack during conflict situations.

Recent efforts by global feminist activists have forced the United Nations to address violence against women in conflict situations. The Beijing Platform for Action has been quite influential in directing the efforts of the international community to prevent violence against women in conflict situations. In addition, feminist theorists offer a new look into violence against women during war by arguing that women's bodies have become the battleground in war, that rape and forced pregnancy used in genocidal campaigns are themselves forms of genocide, and that rape adds layers of complications to the postwar healing.

Rape in war usually involves enemy non-combatants though rape among military personnel also poses a concern for wartime situations. Although both international law and most military codes of conduct have strict prohibitions against targeting non-combatants, rape was and is often overlooked. During World War II, for instance, rape was considered an undesirable but foreseen element of military operations. As deplorable as this attitude is, it is just the tip of the iceberg. Rape is also used in a systematic fashion during war as part of military strategy. In the former Yugoslavia, for instance, human rights organizations reported at least five different ways that rape was used as part of the war effort. First, rape was used to frighten and intimidate a community before the military attack. Then, the Serbs included rape in the strategy to attack and conquer a town or region. They divided populations by sex and age; women were raped or taken prisoner for use in rape camps. Rape camps were buildings taken over for the sole purpose of housing women who were raped repeatedly and regularly for months. The rape camps also served another function. The Serbs believed that a child carried the ethnicity of his or her father so the rape camps were also used to forcibly impregnate women and make them carry the child to term. In this way, rape and forced pregnancy were tools in the campaign for ethnic cleansing. Fourth, rape was perpetrated simply for the sake of rape in the detention and refugee centers. Finally, some women were imprisoned in 'bordello' camps where they were raped repeatedly until they were killed. These uses of rape are not confined to the former Yugoslavia, however. Rape and other forms of sexual abuse are present in every conflict situation and it is primarily women who are the victims.

In a converse fashion, men's bodies become weapons in war. Some of the anecdotal accounts from victims of war rape report men referring to their penises as extensions of or interchangeable with their weapons. There is even a military marching chant that invokes this questionable and troubling confusion of penises and weaponry: 'This is my weapon, this is my gun. With this I shoot bullets, with this I have fun.'

In the early 1990s we witnessed two major genocidal campaigns and both used rape as a principal means of perpetrating genocide. Unfortunately, conflicts in the former Yugoslavia and Rwanda were not the last such campaigns. More recently, rape has been used extensively in the Darfur region of Sudan and the Congo. Feminist theorists studying war rape have argued not just that rape is used as part of genocide but that rape itself is genocide. Genocidal rape is rape that kills. It might be rape that is repeated until the woman dies or rape that is done in a way that kills the woman. Rape is often perpetrated with objects other than the penis with the intent to kill. Some women who live through rapes commit suicide, infanticide, or simply wish they were dead. Genocidal rape – whether as a part of a genocide campaign or as genocide itself – is also systematic and widespread. It is rape perpetrated against a people: an ethnic, cultural, or religious group. But it is also against women, which has led many radical feminists to refer to genocidal rape as femicide – the systematic killing of women.

Rape also poses numerous challenges to the postwar efforts

to establish peace and restore security. The case of Rwanda is illustrative in this regard. During the Rwandan genocide 800,000 people were killed in approximately one hundred days in 1994 – neighbors were frequently raped by their neighbors. Moreover, even after the conflict was over, many victims of rape were killed before they could testify against their former friends and fellow townspeople. Some women were reluctant to even bring charges against their rapists because they feared reprisals. The International Criminal Tribunal for Rwanda (ICTR) faced this and many other challenges. Both the ICTR and the International Criminal Tribunal for the former Yugoslavia (ICTY) added rape and torture to the list of crimes against humanity and the ICTR also added forced pregnancy. In 1997, 'rape as a means of genocide' was added to the charges against Jean-Paul Akayesu, Mayor of Taba, Rwanda, and a year later he became the first man ever tried and convicted of genocide and rape as a crime against humanity.

Such convictions are an important step to the postwar healing. But there are other elements that also need to be addressed. For instance, some cultures have strong prohibitions against any sort of sexual intercourse prior to or outside of marriage. Many of the women who had been raped in the former Yugoslavia and in Rwanda were ostracized by their communities. This is another way in which rape is genocidal – it tears apart communities. In the wake of such tragic experiences, and for the sake of the rape victims and their children, postwar reparations must include adequate attention to the way rape has damaged personal and communal relations. Counseling ought to be provided not just for the women but also for the families of rape victims and the wider community so that rape victims will not continue to feel the pain of their experience from within their own community.

Importantly, feminists and other activists concerned about justice argue that punishment for the perpetrators of rape ought to be part of postwar proceedings. Appropriate tribunals would need to be established within militaries and at the national and international level. This proposal would entail trials for individual soldiers who perpetrated rape as well as trials for officers in charge who stood by and did not stop rape from occurring or who actually included rape in their planning and strategy for the war effort.

Global feminist coalition

A number of global feminist theorists address the possibilities of coalitions among feminists across borders and internationally. Global feminist coalitions have already taken shape in efforts to combat sex trafficking and rape of women during conflict situations. Additional forms of global solidarity among women offer not only promising coalition building but also insightful theoretical analyses of global problems.

Global feminist coalitions require sharing in some political goal but do not require any sort of shared identity or experience. The idea is to unite women because of a shared commitment but maintain the uniqueness of each individual within the coalition. Solidarity here is a political solidarity and contrasts with the call for sisterhood or solidarity in second wave feminism. Second wave feminism looked for shared experiences of oppression or identity to ground sisterhood among women. Global feminists use the language of shared political commitment or, in the words of Chandra Talpade Mohanty, 'common context of struggle.'

In this way, global feminist coalitions can draw on the collective experience of all participants. Often, of course, transnational or global feminist coalitions are formed across borders or in spite of language barriers. Cultural codes and national political regimes may pose problems or obstacles to coalitions.

Sympathetic feminists in one country may find their participation in a cause in another country not welcomed because their government is blameworthy for the pain and suffering of the women and men in that other country. Their efforts should perhaps be redirected toward challenging their own government before they can make alliances and build coalitions with activists in another country.

For example, women in the United States might join forces with women in Sudan or the Congo in efforts to prevent mass rape campaigns. Each participant in the coalition gives to the cause from her unique talents and abilities. All these efforts coalesce in the global feminist political action. Importantly, however, in order for a true coalition – transnational or global solidarity – to form, concrete efforts must be made to listen and learn about the others with whom one is united in solidarity. In addition, cultures and histories matter. As part of our listening, we should also try to ask about the many cultural codes that inform our various approaches to a situation. In that way, we at least try to avoid repeating oppressive or dominant relations in our interactions across borders and around the globe.

Epistemologically, the commitments to global feminist action might require what Maria Lugones calls 'world'-traveling. 'World'-traveling is a metaphor for understanding. When one travels the world literally, one has to make some changes to how one thinks and acts. Real travel often opens up new ways of seeing things because it exposes the traveler to new ideas and perspectives. In the same way, epistemological 'world'-traveling asks us to see others not from our own standpoint but from their standpoint. We are asked to try to understand a person as that person understands her- or himself. 'World'-traveling of this sort entails empathy and real efforts at friendship.

Morally, the commitment to global feminist action means that interpersonal relations and daily decisions are scrutinized for their global impact. The morally right thing to do is not just what would bring about the best consequences for oneself and others in an immediate circle of contacts. Instead, the consequences of our actions are measured globally – so too, do our duties expand globally. The other important moral element to global feminist commitment involves reciprocal agency. Feminists from Canada, the United States, and Europe are not the only ones with agency or the only ones to contribute to feminist theory. Women and men from the Third World, or the two-thirds world, exercise moral agency – the ability to act for their own well-being and the well-being of others – and have quite a lot to contribute to global feminist theory.

One of the most interesting things about transnational and global feminist coalitions is that they reveal that feminists from very different schools of thought and very different methodologies can come together to create significant social change toward the liberation of all women, men, and children. And, in the process, individuals are transformed as well. These are some of the central goals of feminist theory. Like third wave feminism, global feminism shows us that feminism is not just a women's issue.

7

Riding the waves through some feminist issues

In Chapter 1, I presented the 'waves of feminist theory and action' and some of the various interpretations of those waves. The last four chapters have looked at the thematic aspects of first, second, and third wave feminism as well as global feminism. In this chapter, I use this thematic division of the previous four chapters to look at five different issues. These issues help to illustrate at least some of what is at stake for women and how feminism and feminist theory have brought about changes in how we think or what we view as acceptable. Ultimately, as we will see, the three thematic waves rely on each other and work with each other in important ways. While I present each issue using the waves as a guide, the demands of the specific issues discussed often require that the separations between waves of feminist thought and action melt away. Readers are invited to read all five issues but each is also more or less self-contained and thus a cafeteria approach to this chapter – selecting only what one wants – is also appropriate.

Standards of beauty

It certainly will come as no surprise that what counts as beauty is variable and socially or culturally based. Also, standards of beauty for women tend to change much more rapidly than rules of attractiveness for men. These vicissitudes could be driven by market forces seeking to sell the latest fashion, diet, surgery, or what have you. Or there could be other, more subtle forces at work. Perhaps, for instance, standards of beauty are influenced by such things as whether the country is at war. During World War II, women were called upon to work in everything from journalism to munitions production. The image of a strong woman with her hair neatly out of the way and her practical clothes revealing muscle in service to her country (Rosie the Riveter) is an iconic image of beauty for that era. But ten years later, a woman wearing blue jeans would be considered vulgar or low-class. Rosie was replaced with the classic image of house-wife and mother aptly portrayed in television shows. The popularization of television in the 1950s brought an increase in the sheer number of images one might encounter on a daily basis and perhaps contributed to the rapid pace of shifts in the standards of beauty for women.

First wave feminists were primarily concerned with legal and social rights as we have seen but beauty standards certainly played a role as well even if they were not always identified as such. When Sojourner Truth asked 'Ain't I a woman?' as part of the US feminist and abolitionist activities in 1851 she highlighted the disparity between white women and women of color. Her speech pointed to the way white men treat white women – helping them 'out of carriages' and 'over puddles' – and noted that black women are not treated similarly. Implicitly, Sojourner Truth appealed to the different standards of feminin-ity applied when she asked, 'Ain't I a woman?' She was a mother thirteen times over and her muscles testified to long days of labor in the fields. But what makes a woman a woman? Are there certain characteristics that one must have? Should one act a particular way or carry oneself gracefully in order to meet the standards of beauty for women?

Mary Wollstonecraft and Virginia Woolf similarly pointed out how social standards of femininity kept women from full participation in business, political, and academic life. Some first wave feminists adopted new styles of clothing or took to wearing some male styles of clothing as a way to flout the overly restrictive dress, or overly ornate dress, prescribed to women. Of course, as Truth's speech also makes clear, at least some of the feminist concerns about restrictive standards of beauty are particular to upper and middle class women. Working class women did not have the same constraints of femininity because they did not have the resources or leisure to be affected by them.

In the second wave, the critique of standards of beauty began to emphasize the effects of restrictive feminine social prescriptions on women's health and overall acceptance of the female body. For instance, Simone de Beauvoir recounts the effects of conditioning girls in the social dictates of femininity in *The Second Sex*. The young girl is hardly even aware that her body is any different from the bodies of her male friends. But during adolescence, the girl is confronted with a new reality. Not only is her body changing, but according to Beauvoir, the girl also realizes the effects of these changes on her experience of freedom. To become a woman means, at least in part, learning what society expects of you as a woman. Beauvoir discusses a huge array of social expectations, including physical appearance, but unlike the social expectations on boys, the social expectations on girls and women usually inhibit them from acting freely. Clothing and body posture, hair and make-up, voice and diction, manners and skills, are all subject to scrutiny by a society that constantly wants to measure whether a woman is feminine enough.

Another example of second wave emphasis on the effects of social standards of beauty on women's bodies and health may be found in the study and public discussion of eating disorders. Although eating disorders have been around for centuries, public attention did not turn toward them until the latter part of the twentieth century. Largely through the efforts of the women's movement, anorexia and bulimia are now more readily recognized, identified, and treated. Moreover, many feminists have linked eating disorders in some way to the barrage of images of unrealistically thin women in popular media. In a well known documentary series (*Killing us Softly*), Jean Kilbourne demonstrates the image of femininity employed by the advertising industry. Kilbourne's straight-talk message is that the images of woman used in advertising are sexist, unrealistic representations (often airbrushed or otherwise altered to make the women pictured even thinner, tanner, or more full bodied than they already are). Insofar as these images dominate advertising and other popular forms of media, they tyrannize the women who internalize them as the feminine ideal. Eating disorders, excessive dieting, cosmetic plastic surgery and similar practices that aim at altering one's body to conform to socially determined standards greatly affect not only the health of individual women but also the community.

Standards of feminine beauty also affect women of different races and classes differently. Sometimes the standards are set in such a way that only white, wealthy women of European background can possibly 'measure up.' At other times, different images are used that, while not perhaps standards of beauty, nonetheless function to control women. In *Black Feminist Thought* (1990) Patricia Hill Collins discusses four controlling images that affect black women in the United States. The images discussed by Collins are the mammy, the matriarch, the welfare mother, and the jezebel. Each has some roots in the history of slavery and each negatively represents the power and sexuality of black women in a different way. These images function to uphold sexism, racism, and classism by categorizing the behavior of black women and positing a disparaged 'other' for the white, middle class, docile, thin, blue-eyed blonde woman.

Standards of beauty pit light skin against dark and privilege European facial structures over other facial structures. When these standards are internalized, they form a part of a deeply entrenched oppressive system.

Second wave feminism does not just criticize standards of beauty and social practices that adversely affect women. It also works diligently at efforts to embrace the female body as different from the male body. In 1970 the Boston Women's Health Book Collective published the first edition of *Our Bodies, Ourselves*. This groundbreaking book sought to provide accurate information to women about their bodies. Moreover, by continuing to raise awareness about women's health, the Collective has helped to transform how we talk about women's health related issues. In the course of four short decades, we have moved from never mentioning specifically female health related issues to devoting significant research funds and public policy initiatives to target women's health concerns. By giving women permission to explore and know their own bodies, *Our Bodies Ourselves* helped to bring about positive social change that directly impacts women's quality of life.

Third wave feminist theory certainly continues some of the critique of social standards of beauty as well as some of the positive movements toward a balanced, healthy appreciation of the female body found in the second wave. But third wave feminists are quite diverse and celebrate the myriad differences between women. Rather than seeking some commonality among women and women's experience of the body, third wave feminists encourage individual women to live in their bodies in unique and creative ways. Each woman inhabits her body differently but even beyond that, the body might be seen as a sort of canvas upon which one can paint one's own self-proclaimed identity. Whereas many second wave feminists saw plastic surgery and extreme make-up regimes as oppressive, many third wave feminists look upon the body as a means to their personal form of expression. Piercing, tattooing, and transforming the body through surgery or athletic training are seen as displaying one's uniqueness and personality. So too, many third wave feminists even embrace the more traditional standards of femininity arguing that one can be a powerful woman and also display a feminine body. This approach often accompanies a more open or explicit sexuality. That is, third wave feminists argue that women ought to feel empowered to experience and explore their sexuality in whatever ways they desire.

A global feminist approach to standards of beauty focuses on the industries that seem to support and drive those standards. Fashion and beauty constitute a global industry transferring over US$150 billion a year. Of course, the specific standards of beauty being marketed are only rarely culturally sensitive. The Western market of Europe and the United States usually determines what is meant by beauty and what sort of research and development is funded. It is worth pausing to wonder how race and class oppression are maintained within this global industry. Could it be that standards of beauty from the West operate as a sort of neocolonial tool to manipulate cultural ideologies? Do Western images of women have an effect on how women are treated in India, Thailand, China, South Africa, Mali, Brazil, and elsewhere?

Another way to think about the global feminist challenge with regard to standards of beauty is to think about all the possible implications of beauty standards and product purchases. Purchasing products in the United States or Europe often does have some direct or indirect impact on people all over the globe. Global feminism traces at least some of these consequences with regard to the beauty industry. They might, for instance, wonder about the conditions for workers in the plants that produce make-up – especially make-up that contains lead (which was recently divulged as a common ingredient in lipsticks). Global feminists would also look at the wages of the workers. Are the men and women producing beauty products able to provide for the basic needs of themselves and their families?

In addition, ecofeminists would be quick to point out the effects of the beauty industry on the more-than-human-world. In the last few decades, companies have been more open about product labeling and some companies have even advertised that their products are not tested on animals. Of course, there is generally no governmental or industry definition of 'no animal testing' so even the labeling might be deceptive. For an ecofeminist who sees the connection between the oppression of women and the oppression of animals, those sorts of concerns have to be scrutinized for even our most mundane product purchases.

Pregnancy

A first wave approach to pregnancy might begin by noting the role of women in the family and the status of pregnancy in the public or social sphere. Pregnancy has only recently become a widely accepted topic for public discussion and in some cultures it remains a taboo subject. It does not take much digging to uncover the many euphemisms that were used to avoid talking directly about pregnancy or birth: in a delicate condition, bun in the oven, with child, visit from the stork, ready to pop, knocked up, eating for two, in a family way, awaiting the tax deduction, and, of course, preggers. There are also more subtle language issues with childbirth or pregnancy. Consider, for instance, the common expression that the 'doctor delivers the baby.' A woman who has given birth might find this expression rather troubling given the 'labor' that she exerts in the process.

Why is it that we avoid speaking about something so common as pregnancy and childbirth? Perhaps it has something to do with the fact that it is done exclusively by women. If men are setting the political agenda or determining health policy then a condition that affects solely women is not likely to rise to the top of the list of topics needing attention. First and second wave feminists confronted this fact head on by working to make pregnancy and childbirth not only accepted topics for public debate and discussion but also by claiming women's rights and reproductive power.

Feminists have worked to revalue the role of mothers in society and take heed of the important training of young children that mothers do from infancy. This entails an acknowledgment of the unique knowledge and skill that mothers exhibit in rearing children.

Feminists also argued for recognition of the toll pregnancy takes on the female body. The women's movement is the single most important movement to change workplace habits and policies in order to allow greater participation at all levels of industry of women who mother. Although there are still many barriers to break before we can say that women are in fact equal in the workplace, having federally mandated maternity or family leave has certainly contributed to women breaking through many glass ceilings. Moreover, many companies today not only meet the family leave requirements but have embraced family-friendly policies with on-site daycare, flex-time, private nursing rooms, and paid or unpaid leave for elder care.

If we use the waves of feminist theory to try to make sense of the social changes around the issue of pregnancy and child-birth, we would begin by acknowledging the contributions that came from changes in the law regarding women's right to vote. Through the struggle to obtain suffrage, feminist activists found political power in their united efforts as well as in their new found ability to influence local and national policy. First wave feminist theory rarely addresses pregnancy directly but it does address family structure. Their roles as childbearers and as mothers of citizens give women at least some incentive to challenge their lack of participation in political life and the lack of attention to women's issues in political life.

In the second wave, feminists add a focus on the body and challenge society to examine the effects of social policy and customs on the female body in reproduction. Perhaps the most prominent challenge is the debate over a woman's right to choose to continue her pregnancy or to abort the fetus. Even before abortion was part of political discourse, though, birth control was.

It is estimated that half a million women die each year from childbirth. In addition, many women are forced, coerced, or cajoled into having more pregnancies than they wish or more frequent pregnancies than is healthy. Reproductive freedom means global access to the tools to freely choose when and where to have children. Contraception is just one possible tool. Increased access to higher levels of education that have been shown to delay a woman's first pregnancy and thus the overall number of pregnancies she has in a lifetime is another. Adequate prenatal and postnatal care are additional tools in the arsenal of reproductive freedom because if we can reduce the rate of early childhood mortality, we will reduce the number of children a woman has.

The availability of contraception has a long and storied past. It is often tied up with political interests or religious commitments. Nevertheless, the development and provision of safe, adequate birth control for women has long been a feminist cause. It contributes to women's health and well-being; supports women's empowerment in work, politics, and home; and transforms cultural or social expectations for females. Arguably, birth control also makes every child into a chosen, desired child. But accompanying efforts to ensure appropriate maternal nutrition and care for fetal health should a woman choose to become pregnant ought also to be seen as crucial to feminist arguments regarding reproductive freedom. That freedom, after all, also means the freedom to have children in a supportive environment.

Another important aspect of the childbirth experience is lactation. The social acceptance and appreciation of nursing mothers has changed dramatically in the last forty years. While debate still rages about the health benefits of breast milk versus formula and nursing in public, more women feel they have a choice in whether or not to nurse their babies. Moreover, adoptive parents and fathers are also exploring how they can participate in the process of delivering breast milk to new born infants thanks in part to the advances made by the feminist movement.

Beyond the abortion and lactation debates, though, second wave feminism also brought about tremendous changes in the medical field. A vast majority of the world's women do not have adequate prenatal care or access to safe birthing methods. By reclaiming control of woman's body in social thought and medical practice, second wave feminists help to transform the birth process. Accurate, honest, and relatively complete information about women's bodies is much more publically available thanks in part to the women's movement worldwide. By empowering individual women with knowledge of their bodies – including detailed information about sex, menstruation, pregnancy, childbirth, lactation, and menopause – such frank discussions give women new expertise when they visit their doctors and allow them to take control of their own health as never before. Second wave feminist theory argued that women were not like men and to treat them as such was not only demeaning, it was potentially hazardous to their health. The birthing experience now is quite different than it was even just ten years ago. Many hospitals accommodate a variety of birth plans such as bathtub births, intimate birthing rooms, midwives, and natural or assisted birth. And the international community has gained greater appreciation for the needs of pregnant women and nursing mothers.

Pregnancy and childbirth are celebrated in the second wave. Some feminists see in them a special power that women have or a special connection to their biological children. Others simply celebrate the fact that pregnancy is out of the closet and visible in television and movies, or discussed in the workplace and at the highest levels of government. But not every woman experiences pregnancy and, among those who do, they do not experience pregnancy, childbirth, or motherhood in the same way. If we want to do justice to women's experiences, we need to acknowledge the important differences even as we also seek solidarity among feminists to bring about social change. Women of different classes, races, body-types, ages, and cultural backgrounds will experience pregnancy differently. Whereas early second wave feminism made women's experience public and challenged aspects of that experience that were oppressive, late second wave feminism had to acknowledge the interconnections between other forms of oppression and how those interconnections impacted our understanding of sexism.

bell hooks argues that familial relations are one of the primary places where people learn domination and subordination. If those relations are also affected by racism or other forms of powerlessness, then the experience of motherhood will undoubtedly be different than the starry-eyed picture often presented in popular media on the subject. Moreover, as we saw in Chapter 4, pregnancy itself might be a conflicted experience that includes some symbolic reminder of the racist past where black women's bodies were used by slave masters.

It is important that pregnancy or motherhood not be used to define or characterize all women. Some second and third wave feminists call into question the assumptions surrounding biological motherhood. They challenge the often spoken claim that biological mothers have a bond with their children that develops even before the child is born. Bonds with children are not natural but chosen they argue; they must be fostered and nurtured. Biological connections are not necessary or sufficient for the connection between parents and children. Rather, mothering takes many forms and comes from many different people. By challenging this biological or natural assumption, the way is opened for rethinking the bonds of adoptive parents, fathers, gay and lesbian parents, foster parents, co-parents, and other familial arrangements. Social change often begins when our long-held assumptions are unseated. Once we understand that biological mothers need not be the only people doing mothering work in society, so the argument goes, we begin to recognize the real possibilities for new social arrangements.

Third wave feminism adds another interesting twist to our conceptions of pregnancy and childbirth. Pregnancy in the third wave is also celebrated but in a different sort of way. It is much more personal and public at the same time. Pregnancy fashion and the beautiful pregnant body are embraced not only for their import socially and politically but also for their sensuality. The pregnant body is no longer hidden in baggy clothing but is prominently displayed on magazine covers. (While pregnant, Demi Moore famously posed for the cover of *Vanity Fair* magazine in 1991. Although controversial, this cover has been described as empowering insofar as it showed the pregnant body as sexy.)

Another contribution from third wave feminism is the symbolic use of the pregnant or lactating body. Hélène Cixous, prominent French feminist, speaks of writing with white ink in her discussion of feminine writing. She challenges women to write in a way that subverts the dominant masculine way of writing. This *l'écriture feminine* even involves writing in a way that undermines or resists rules of grammar. By doing so, women open up a place for themselves outside the world that men have constructed. Writing in white ink is a specifically feminine way of writing that rejects the masculine norms. White ink is metaphorically associated with breast milk. Breast milk is important here because of its connection to the abject body –

the body that repulses as it attracts. Women and women's bodies have been the abject body in Western culture. In order for women to 'write themselves' outside of the dominant culture, to create themselves outside the oppressive influence of masculinity and masculine social structures, women must claim and embrace their abject bodies.

Global feminism also contributes to the ongoing feminist activism regarding pregnancy, childbirth, mothering, and the family. As we saw in the previous chapter, one of the issues in global feminism is the global care chain. Wealthy women from one nation often buy the services of poorer women from another nation. These poorer women frequently leave their own children behind in the hopes of providing a better life for them by sending money back home. In addition to this global care chain, we could also speak about surrogacy and forced pregnancy. Surrogacy is a practice whereby one woman gives birth for another woman. The contracting woman might provide the egg (and her partner the sperm) or the surrogate might be the egg provider while the sperm comes from the contracting potential father. Surrogacy is contracting for someone else to be pregnant for you. It is a controversial practice for a number of different reasons. One reason global feminists are concerned about surrogacy is that wealthy women rarely contract other wealthy women to carry their babies. Rather, it is the poor who are solicited for this practice and the risk for exploitation is very high. (Of course, surrogacy is also legitimately used on a voluntary basis when close relatives or friends agree to carry a child for a woman unable to do so.) A global feminist account of pregnancy would scrutinize the global structure of childbirth and healthcare distribution in an effort to uncover all the ways poor people in less developed nations are exploited or abused by their own countries and by individuals in nations in wealthier regions of the world.

Forced pregnancy is a practice that uses rape in war for the purposes of ethnic cleansing and/or genocide. Both the

Rwandan and the Yugoslav war crimes tribunals found that systematic campaigns of rape had been used. Women's bodies became the site for combat. Raping the women and girls of a community had multiple effects. It demoralized the community as well as the soldiers who heard stories of their wives, sisters, daughters, and mothers being raped. The tribunals further found that in many cases women became pregnant from the rapes and were forced to remain in rape camps until their pregnancies were to term. Pregnancy, in other words, is often used as a tool for manipulation and violence.

Rape

Rape is a central issue that shapes women's experiences. Rape affects not only the individual who is raped but also her family, her community, and perhaps even all women. The different feminist approaches to rape reveal these various sides to the issue as well as highlight some of the ways that rape shapes the identity and agency of the women who are victimized.

First wave feminism focuses on legal and moral rights. It stands to reason, then, that first wave feminism would focus its efforts regarding rape on changing laws to protect women and prosecute rapists. Four central components of this focus are: (1) challenge the status of women as men's property, (2) redefine or reconceptualize legal definitions of rape, (3) change a legal system that revictimizes the rape victim, and (4) prosecute the rapist and deter other possible rapists. These are ongoing efforts. Women are still seen as the property of their closest male relative in some countries, and rape is understood as a natural male response. In such contexts, women who put themselves in a position of being alone with a non-relative male could expect to be raped. Moreover, legal systems all over the world continue to struggle with how to prosecute rape accounting for particular social and cultural expectations as well as protecting the rights of all parties involved. A recent case in Saudi Arabia raised all of these issues and garnered the attention of the international community. A woman was gang raped by seven men for being in a car with a male who was not a relative. She was initially sentenced to ninety lashings but the courts changed it to two hundred lashings and six months in prison. Four of her rapists were also convicted and sentenced to jail time and lashings. This case illustrates not only the revictimization of the rape victim in the court system but, given the initial lenient sentences for the rapists, it also illustrates the trouble feminists face in changing how society perceives men's rights regarding women and handles rape cases.

Early law pertaining to rape in Western countries held that it was a violation of a man's property in the person of his wife or daughter. In such a context, the crime was against another man, not against the woman who was the actual target of the violation. The next step was to define or redefine rape. Rape had to be moved from being a property crime to being a personal crime and in doing so the definition of rape in many jurisdictions became penetration by a penis and ejaculation. But this is a very limited understanding of rape. People have been raped with all kinds of objects and ejaculation seems a rather arbitrary standard by which to determine whether penetration by a penis is rape. The implications are astounding: a woman might be penetrated by a penis or, in the case of gang rape, multiple penises and yet her attacker or attackers would not be charged with rape but with some lesser crime such as assault; a woman might have a bottle, a knife, even a gun forced into her vagina and yet the perpetrator might be charged with battery but not rape; examples like these abound. A related implication of definitions of rape as penetration and ejaculation is that sex becomes defined by or focused on the activity of the penis. Women's sexual experience and pleasure are insignificant according to such an account.

Following the changes in the laws and concepts of rape, first and second wave feminists argue that the legal system must be transformed so as to avoid revictimizing women who have been raped. Women are often forced to relive the experience of rape in a cold or even hostile courtroom environment. If their sexual histories become part of the trial proceedings, even when the sexual histories of the perpetrator (including sexual histories of violent crime) are protected, then something is amiss. Even when a woman who has been raped manages to bring her case to trial, the chances of the rapist being convicted remain slim.

Finally, first wave feminism has to break through a substantial protective barrier that often keeps perpetrators of rape from being brought to trial. Susan Brownmiller argues that patriarchy forms a sort of allegiance among men such that they become blind to the faults of their fellows and protect them even in spite of recognizing criminal behavior. Male police officers might fail to arrest a man who is accused by his wife of rape, male prosecutors might be more lenient on a man accused of rape because of his status in the community, and even among strangers there may be some unspoken bond that allows or requires men to overlook bad behavior in other men. The military still struggles with this issue; women in the military often risk additional violence or retribution from superiors for trying to report that a male colleague raped them.

Second wave feminism engages in a lively debate about rape and how best to understand its place in contemporary culture. Two main sides of the debate may be represented by Brownmiller on one side and Catharine MacKinnon and Andrea Dworkin on the other. The question is whether rape is about power or about sex. MacKinnon and Dworkin describe sex and violence as 'mutually definitive.' They famously offered a definition of rape that appears to include any sexual intercourse that occurs within a system of male dominance. In other words, heterosexual intercourse within a sexist social system would also be included under the umbrella concept of rape. Rape is about sex. Pornography and prostitution would also be included or otherwise classed as sexual violation insofar as they are sexual relations occurring under coercion or displaying dominance. It is important to note at this point that MacKinnon and Dworkin do think that equal sexual relations are possible – they even discuss what non-dominating erotica might look like – but the social conditions that keep women oppressed must be altered in order for such a positive equality of sexuality to be possible.

Brownmiller argues that rape is not an act of sex but rather an act of power. Rape is violent and to call it sex misses that point. She further suggests that rape is used as a more or less intentional system of intimidation insofar as it keeps all women in fear for their safety and security. Like MacKinnon and Dworkin, Brownmiller sees prostitution and pornography as forms of rape but for her the emphasis is that they too are based on domination and coercion – that they are sex is really secondary. Rape is about power. All three feminists are considered radical because they argue that the oppression of women is the fundamental form of oppression regardless of whether we understand that as built on power or sex.

Although I have been speaking of rape as if it only happens to women, the fact is that anyone can be raped. The feminists discussed here, however, argue that rape is against 'women'; in that case, when men and boys are raped, they are perceived as occupying or forced to assume the weaker position in society, they are, in effect, made to be 'women.'

The argument over whether rape is about power or sex may seem rather trivial or academic, especially to victims of rape. Nevertheless, taking a position in this controversy informs the practical strategies feminists use to change public attitudes about rape, rapists, and rape victims. In addition, both MacKinnon and Brownmiller show that rape is part of a system of dominance, whether as a tool that sustains dominance or as a result of it, rape manifests the oppression of women in a particularly violent manner.

Date rape, the rape of a person by an acquaintance that may or may not include marks of physical violence beyond the sexual intercourse, and spousal rape, the rape by one's spouse or intimate partner, gained legal status in the later part of the twentieth century in many jurisdictions because of the work of feminist theorists and activists. Although date rape continues to be controversial and some women have used it in an abusive manner, these are continued steps to try to protect women from sexual violence.

Some second wave and third wave feminist theorists take a more individualized approach to rape, in contrast to – or in conjunction with – the political or politicized methods of MacKinnon, Dworkin, and Brownmiller. For instance, some argue that women internalize the ideology of rape and this internalization shapes everything from bodily comportment to moral agency. By living in fear, women may carry themselves in more guarded, less open ways. Women might think about themselves as rapeable which, in turn, affects personal identity as well as personal choice and action. In this way, the threat of rape contributes to the psychological oppression discussed in Chapter 4.

Another third wave contribution to the theoretical understandings of rape pertains to the discourses about rape. Discourse, here, comprises the specialized linguistic tools that shape how we think about a topic. The discourse on rape might be said to produce the feminine body: it defines and delimits women's bodies as vulnerable and penetrable. The idea of rape or the threat of rape lays hold of our imaginations and informs women of their place in a power structure.

Finally, third wave feminist theory also highlights the different meanings of rape given the intersections of race, class, and gender. The history of rape's use in slavery, for instance, to make women submissive, destroy the morale of slave families, and add to the master's slave holdings, affects how rape is experienced and understood for women of color. Feminism needs to pay attention to these intersections of oppressions.

Economic coercion and social status also play important roles in the personal and social understanding of rape. It is still the case that prostitutes in many jurisdictions have difficulty convincing police and court personnel to take their cases of rape seriously. Even a quick survey of how rape is covered by popular media reveals a social disparity regarding the treatment of victims and the seriousness of the crime. White women from the middle and upper classes are treated as sympathetic victims while lower class women, women of color, immigrant women, and other women whose social status is less secure are often considered as blame-worthy in some way.

Global feminist accounts discuss rape as a tool of politics and a weapon in conflict situations, as discussed in the previous chapter. Rape divides communities. Women become the battle-field of war and the site for a culture under siege. Many of the most far-reaching global feminist efforts have targeted violence against women and sexual violence almost always takes center stage.

Domestic violence

Not so long ago it was an accepted and perhaps even expected part of marriage that men could dominate their wives and children, even with violence if they deemed it necessary. Jean-Jacques Rousseau even suggests that women be raised in a way that prepares them for the ill temper of their future husbands. The law in Britain and the United States, by protecting the 'sanctity of the home' turned a blind eye to abuses that might occur therein. This societal split between public life and private life was meant to protect individual liberty – to allow each person or each family to pursue their own version of the good life.

The public face of the family, that is, the voice of the family in public and political life was represented by the husband/father/master. The domestic sphere – or private life – was commonly understood as a sort of mini-kingdom. (Certainly there are many colloquial expressions that uphold this understanding: 'A man's home is his castle' and 'the sanctity of the home.') Even in contemporary law enforcement, police have long been reluctant to intervene in familial disputes of any kind. The home is a protected space and the various branches of the state, it was presumed, ought to stay out.

But in practice, this sharp division between the private/domestic/familial sphere and the public/political/legal sphere prove to be quite perilous for many women and children and not just in the West. Honor killings in the Middle East and South Asia, violence and murder against women in China, and unreported physical and mental abuse in Japan are some of the many examples of violence against intimate partners worldwide.

Social beliefs about the proper role of the wife and mother further support a man's right to rule his home according to whatever means he deems appropriate. In many social and legal contexts in the world, a wife enjoys no independent legal rights. She is merely a part of the property of a man. (Friedrich Engels, an early Marxist feminist, argues that the root of the word *family* is *familus* or domestic slave. The number of slaves a man owned was referred to as *familia*.) Although women's status in the family has changed to some extent in Europe and the US, the traditional Western marriage ceremony still reveals some of these roots. A father walks his daughter down the aisle and hands her over to her soon-to-be-husband. The transfer of property is understood as a contract – the marriage contract – and is, in some cultures (Western and non-Western alike) accompanied by an exchange of money as well. Furthermore, by teaching women that a 'woman's place is in the home' and that 'two parents are better than one,' social values ensure a certain amount of submissiveness by many women. Women who find themselves seemingly trapped in a violent relationship might face hopelessness or despair given such overwhelming social messages that 'they made their beds and now they must lie in them.'

As should be evident, there are numerous varieties of feminism. Many of them suggest approaches for challenging the unjust social arrangement of women in domestic violence situations. Some feminists target what they identify as the roots of the problem in ideological sex roles, others target a culture of violence, and others seek the source in unequal legal and social rights for women. Continuing with the thematic waves of feminist theory, we can see some of the variety of approaches that have been pursued and continue to be pursued.

First wave methods of addressing the problem of violence by men against women in the home include naming the social phenomena, identifying the laws that allow it to continue and proposing new laws that protect women in the home. The first of these, naming the social phenomena, is more significant than it might appear at first blush. Women often suffer isolation and a sense of failure when they are victimized by domestic violence. Unless or until women start to identify some similarities in their experiences they will continue to think of it as their individual problem. Naming the problem of domestic violence marks a transition from a private problem to a social problem. Once it has been named, then an individual woman might more readily recognize her own experience in the social problem described by others and begin to take the steps to get out of an abusive relationship. So too, once the naming has occurred, society as a whole is made responsible. The naming forces legislators and policy makers, pastors, psychologists and social workers, and many others to seek to understand how violence affects those they work with and for. It also charges all of us with the task of social transformation in order to create a society free of violence in the home.

It is worth noting that the particular task of naming domestic violence underwent significant modifications and continues to be refined as we understand more about the situation and agency of men and women in relationships. Among the names for the phenomenon I am calling 'domestic violence' are wife battering and spousal abuse. Similarly, those who suffer this abuse have been called battered women, victims, and once they have left an abusive relationship, survivors. Some of these labels acknowledge a woman's agency more directly than others. Advocates working with women who have been abused recognize that naming that fails to recognize and validate a woman's own power and agency just contributes to the abuse.

In identifying the laws that pertain to domestic violence, first wave feminist efforts really began with the laws allowing women to divorce. In some places, women were given the right to divorce in the late eighteenth century, but even late into the twentieth century in the United States the woman often had to prove grounds for divorce which complicated efforts to get out of an abusive relationship. In addition, since domestic violence is often accompanied by controlling behavior, women in abusive relationships might not have access to money to provide for themselves and their children should they leave. Changing the laws that pertain to property ownership and control within the family is crucial to providing adequate alternatives to the abuse.

Perhaps the most important laws that were changed as a result of feminist efforts were those that allowed a man to chastise his wife. English Common Law, for instance, had a rule (often referred to as the 'rule of thumb' from which we get a common phrase) that said a man could punish his wife with a switch – stick – no greater than the thickness of his thumb.

In the second wave, domestic violence was recognized not just as a violation of rights and bodily integrity but also as a significant factor in shaping a woman's agency and identity. One of the most prominent ways that second wave feminism acts is through reporting domestic violence nationally and devising methods to deal with the psychological toll it takes. Japan conducted a nationwide survey in the early 1990s revealing the extent of the problem and owning it as a social ill. Other countries have taken similar steps to report the prevalence of domestic abuse, its root causes, and social effects. In the case of South Africa, for instance, some have speculated that the history of apartheid laid the foundations for a culture of violence and that deep systemic changes must be made in order to encourage adequate reporting of domestic abuse. But South Africa is far from alone. The cycle of violence described by Lenore Walker illustrates just how difficult it is to challenge domestic violence individually and socially.

As Walker describes it, the cycle of violence starts when batterers inflict physical, psychological, or sexual harm on someone with whom they are intimately involved. Perhaps it is a wife or a girlfriend. Walker initially studied heterosexual couples but her theory has been useful in understanding violence in all intimate relations. The initial abuse, according to the cycle theory, is followed by what Walker referred to as the 'honeymoon' period. Honeymoons are blissful times when one partner looks past the faults of another partner. In the case of domestic violence, the person who perpetrated the violence is often very loving and contrite. This stage reinforces the hope and trust in a relationship in spite of the history of violence that marred it. Batterers will often promise that they will never hit their loved one again and the person who has been victimized by violence, perhaps out of love or a desire to salvage the relationship or perhaps for the sake of children, agrees to continue the relationship. The third stage in the cycle is marked by tension building.

At this stage, minor incidents probably do not result in violent outbursts but they certainly contribute to the eventual eruption of violence that starts the cycle again. It is as if the abuser is keeping track of every false step or mistake. The person victimized by violence might walk on eggshells to try to ease the tension or might, alternatively, deliberately do something to bring out the eruption of violence to get it over with.

The cycle theory of violence also validates something that many women have known all along – that violence is not always physical. Domestic violence also includes sexual, emotional, and psychological abuse or neglect. Activists and theorists in the second wave did quite a lot to advance our understanding of these phenomena. Emotional abuse might include such things as isolating a woman from her friends and family. An abusive husband might forbid a woman to speak to her former friends out of jealousy or control. He might also withhold love or emotional support as a way to play on her vulnerability and dependence. The psychological abuse often precedes the physical abuse as the husband or lover more or less systematically tears down his partner's self-esteem. In this way, domestic violence becomes embedded in a woman's picture of herself. She internalizes the psychological abuse and emotional isolation, often concluding that she *is* everything that her abusive partner calls her.

By extending the analysis of the patterns and effects of domestic violence to aspects of a person's identity, second wave feminism paved the way for a larger social movement against domestic violence. The most notable facet of this movement, perhaps, is the shelter movement. Domestic violence shelters first emerged in the 1970s. They are safe havens in secret locations where trained personnel staff a hotline and help women who have been abused. The women are given a short stay in the shelter and assistance navigating the social services to get independent housing, job training, welfare, healthcare, and other provisions to live on their own. Most shelters also have support groups that help women make the personal transition to identifying their experience and reclaiming their self-esteem and empowerment.

But, of course, not every woman has the same social position. Wealthy women might opt to stay in hotels rather than shelters, and rural women might not want to relocate to a city where the nearest shelter is located. Other factors also may make a woman's experience of domestic violence more or less difficult and may make her escape from that situation more or less plausible. Third wave feminists draw our attention to these facts and critique models of feminist theory that fail to account for how race, class, sexuality, disability, and other factors enter into the experience of domestic violence. Kimberlé Crenshaw advocates 'intersectional thinking' when dealing with issues like domestic violence and rape. She notes that domestic violence advocates often failed to understand the impact of racism on the lives of some women who also experienced violence from an intimate partner. Moreover, they also often overlooked the importance of family ties in some women's lives or the nuances of cultural codes in how one reports violence. In that way, domestic violence advocates risk failing to see how race and the violence of racism may be a more pressing concern for some women than the violence they suffer in the domestic sphere. This is presented in the language of 'discourse,' which means the language and specialized knowledge of domestic violence advocacy.

In a similar way, Crenshaw noted how anti-racist politics often left unquestioned the patriarchal social hierarchies and systems of domination that relegated women to vulnerable positions in the home. As a result of the convergence of these two discourses – anti-racist discourse and anti-domestic violence discourse – and the way they both overlooked significant factors in some women's lives, many women of color who were victimized by domestic violence found themselves on the margins. Both campaigns were set up to aid their liberation and neither one adequately understands the situation of oppression.

Intersectionality or intersectional thinking is the type of thinking that Crenshaw proposes to overcome these obstacles. The aim is to map the convergence of racism and patriarchy in how we conceptualize domestic violence. In other words, to use the experience of women of color as a starting point in order to uncover the various systems of domination that converge and intersect. In this way, theory becomes much more complicated and less universalizing but also potentially more insightful into the lives of individual women.

Another third wave insight into domestic violence is the way a woman subjectively experiences her relationship with her abuser. It is often assumed that a person would hate anyone who harms her on a regular basis. Paradoxically, however, many women in domestic violence relationships genuinely love and care for the person doing them harm. This love may be based on 'what used to be' – the love that was present when the relationship was first initiated – or it could be an abiding, continuing, even growing love. A person can love another individual and not like or approve of that individual's actions. By emphasizing subjectivity rather than shared experience or commonality of experience, third wave feminists can address the unique aspects of each person's experience of abuse.

Global feminists, too, offer insight into the problem of domestic violence. Two of the primary endeavors are to get security in the private sphere recognized as a human right and spousal rape recognized as a violation of human rights. Some global feminists, like Uma Narayan, have also noted the link between dowry deaths – murder of a new bride by her husband as a way to steal the dowry – and domestic violence. Narayan's account of women who die from domestic violence takes us back to the importance of *naming*. She notes that dowry deaths have received a considerable amount of attention in the global feminist movement and rightly so. In contrast, however, the deaths of women at the hands of abusive partners or spouses receive relatively little attention. Perhaps part of the reason for this, she suggests, is because there is no politically motivating name for the latter.

In addition, global and transnational feminists have called attention to mail order brides, immigrant marriages, and other cross-nationality unions. When violence is part of these intimate relationships, additional problems intersect with the problem of violence. The situation of mail order brides is often quite precarious. Their contracting husbands may confiscate their passports – if they even have a passport: they could, after all, be brought to a country as part of a human trafficking ring – or refuse to give them any money which might afford them certain freedoms. In these cases, a spouse may be dependent upon her husband for her immigrant status, there may be linguistic barriers that leave her isolated and unable to seek help from shelters or law enforcement personnel, or she may be fearful of greater retribution should she bring any public attention to the union at all.

Clearly, there is still much work to be done to combat domestic violence but the widely different approaches of feminist theorists from all over the globe continue to bring attention to this important issue and make positive change to address and eliminate violence from the home.

Domestic labor

A classic stereotype of feminists is that they refuse to do housework. Housework is just one of those things that has to be done, though, of course, it can be done in a variety of different ways, shared equitably among members of a household, and with varying expectations for its quality. There certainly have been feminists who have refused to do housework and many more who have thought about the distribution of the household responsibilities.

> 'By the millennium, housework should have been abolished. In a sane world, meaningless repetition of non-productive activity would be seen to be a variety of obsessive-compulsive disorder. People who said that they enjoyed doing housework, or needed to do it, or that doing it made them feel good would be known as addicts. Once the word got out that a person was cleaning her toilet every day, therapists would come to her house and reclaim her for rationality and the pleasure principle.'
>
> Germaine Greer, *The Whole Woman* (2002)

First wave feminists are primarily concerned with arguing for the equality of women, as we discussed in Chapter 3. But many of the prominent feminists discussed here did not seriously consider unsettling the gender roles within the home. As wife and mother, there were simply certain duties that women were supposed to perform. Many of these duties were directly related to natural abilities, such as nursing infants, but most were only assumed to be natural to women. Alternative distributions of household chores were rarely considered. Nevertheless, some did suggest paying a wage for housework or otherwise valuing the contribution women in the home make to the overall economy.

It is also worth noting that implicit in the arguments of first wave feminists is a classist position. Consider the feminist arguments in the nineteenth and early twentieth century. The struggle for equal consideration as a rational human being, the fight for suffrage, and the pleas for equal access to the same quality of education that men receive were only one side of the issue of equality. Many women were 'equal' to the men of their class insofar as they also worked long hours in poor working conditions for very low wages. Housework is a luxury when one lives off subsistence wages in the age of industrialism. Women who have to work long hours for low wages find it hard to sympathize with stay-at-home women who are troubled by housework. Although there are still necessary tasks to keep a home running – cooking, providing clothing, tending wounds and ailments – the working class in the late nineteenth century and early twentieth century were more likely to identify their struggles with economic injustice rather than sexist injustice.

As we saw in Chapters 2 and 3, many Marxist and socialist feminists offered varying proposals for how to redistribute housework or reconceptualize domestic labor as a way to extend economic rights to women. These strategies have both first and second wave characteristics. In the second wave, feminists began to question the natural association of motherhood with household obligations. Perhaps women were not destined to be the homemakers. Perhaps there might be a sharing of tasks within the home. For the Marxist and socialist feminist debate on domestic labor, the key question was how to accomplish this redistribution of household obligations. Arguing that all women do housework, they proposed paying women for housework or socializing housework so that it is a shared, state funded activity. Tied in with this, was the question of reproductive labor – housework itself might be considered reproductive labor insofar as it helps to reproduce the next generation of workers. Childcare and elder care, then, are also aspects of housework or domestic labor. Liberal feminists, in contrast, shy away from economic proposals and instead suggest that men be encouraged to share more equitably in the childcare and housework duties.

Simone de Beauvoir, considered the mother of second wave feminism, wrote about housework as she described the life situation of women. Beauvoir compares the endless repetition of the present to the torture of Sisyphus. This description places housework among oppressive practices but Beauvoir did not think that it is necessarily oppressive. It is so only when the houseworker is stuck in the present moment and unable to take on projects that reach into or impact the future. According to Beauvoir, there is little real satisfaction in the completion of the repetitive tasks done in the home; they often lack a purpose greater than themselves. One does dishes in order to use them, get them dirty, and wash them again – and the same holds true for most housework tasks. Moreover, housework according to Beauvoir is busy-work or drudgery that keeps a woman from realizing her own existence and her own freedom. Beauvoir argues that the houseworker should also perform creative or productive work to integrate housework into the course of life. In that case, housework would not be an end in itself but would be merely a passing activity that makes the pursuit of other projects somewhat easier.

Again, though, Beauvoir and other second wave feminists who seek to find commonality in women's experiences of housework are criticized for failing to account for differences among women – especially differences in class and race status. Upper and middle class women might experience what Betty Friedan called the 'feminine mystique' – a feeling a dissatisfaction with life. Such feelings might be exacerbated with the introduction of labor saving devices such as dishwashers and clothes washers and driers (to say nothing of microwaves). As Friedan argued, if a woman is raised by society to believe that her destiny is in making a home for her family, and if the labor involved in doing so takes only a part of her time, she is either left creating new projects (and probably being a good consumer in the process thereby feeding the capitalist system that wants some portion of the population as unpaid laborers) or left feeling empty and useless. However, of course, not every woman or every family has the luxury of an income that would allow someone to stay at home caring for the house and family needs.

Some critics of white, middle class feminism suggest that the focus on the home and patriarchy misses the point. Instead, feminist theory ought to work on transforming the social and political structures that breed systems of alienation, exclusion, domination, and oppression. In addition, there might be some positive theory building that highlights the loving, co-operative possibilities in the home. Some versions of the ethics of care certainly exemplify this theoretical move. It is a shift away from what is wrong with the family structure toward what can be learned by an expansive understanding of diverse familial structures and bonds. Some other examples of this sort of theory include feminist epistemologies that see new understandings emerge through the productive and reproductive domestic labor. Nancy Hartsock's 'feminist standpoint' and Sara Ruddick's 'maternal thinking' (discussed earlier) demonstrate the sort of epistemological efforts that look for insights for theory from within familial structures. With a different aim in mind, bell hooks envisions love as central to new conceptions of social organization.

There are many third wave approaches to domestic labor but just two are highlighted here: domestic labor as resistance and housework as feminist. Second wave feminists might argue that refusing to do housework is a form of political resistance to patriarchal gender roles. A third wave approach to housework as resistance resists the patriarchy and the prescribed roles by embracing new roles and perhaps even embracing contradictory roles. Luce Irigaray, for instance, proposes women 'mime the mimes,' that is, women are to take the 'mimes' or socially constructed gender roles that men have imposed on women and exaggerate them. She thinks that by revealing how ridiculous the 'feminine' is both to ourselves and to other men and women, we take an important step toward liberation. The other aspect of this is that not only are the gender roles prescribed by a sexist system, so too are the rules of logic that demand some consistency. Irigaray suggests that the very act of a feminist acting feminine is a form of rebellion: it displays the self-contradiction in the face of a system that demands logical consistency.

Another third wave approach to housework or domestic labor is that housework is feminist. In a way, this too is a method of embracing opposites or contradictions but it is also linked to the first wave feminist goals of obtaining equal rights. If, as many people believe, feminism is about equality, equal rights, and the right to choose one's own destiny rather than have that destiny determined by patriarchal social roles, then anyone ought to be able to choose to do housework if that is what she or he desires.

Perhaps as a part of this, some women have claimed a leisure status befitting the starlets portrayed in Hollywood films. We might call this a sort of pseudo-feminism that uses the notions of freedom and equality for women at the heart of feminism to pursue one's own self-interest without care for the effects on other women. Pseudo-feminists claim the name 'feminist' but do not adopt a feminist political agenda or work for liberation from oppression of any sort. They generally do not work but they nevertheless hire poorer women to care for their children and do their housework. This allows them ample leisure time to modify their bodies through physical training, make-up, or plastic surgery, and cultivate social ties that might increase their overall social status. It goes without saying that this use of 'feminism' is understood by many feminists who do engage in political action to bring about social change as an abuse of the concept. It also goes without saying that only relatively wealthy women could possibly engage in pseudo-feminism.

Global and transnational feminist approaches to domestic labor, as we saw in the previous chapter, emphasize the impact of poverty on households and discuss the implications of the global caregiver. More broadly, global and transnational feminists discuss the effect of national and international political policies on women and children, family structures, and health and welfare in the home.

* * *

The different feminist approaches to some of the most pressing women's issues reveal only a slice of the rich diversity of feminist theories. True, feminists do not always agree about what the best strategies for liberation might be or even how to best understand what is at stake in any given issue. But there is a lot to be learned from the different approaches and feminists from all schools of thought, waves, and tactics are getting better at listening to each other. Feminists are also making greater efforts to connect the cause of feminism with the causes of other oppressed peoples and other advocates for liberation. Feminism will continue to develop and respond to ever new problems. If the future is anything like the past, we can be assured that feminism will continue to make a significant contribution to efforts to create positive social change and bring about social justice.

Suggested reading

Chapter 1

Banks, O. 1990. *Becoming a Feminist: The Social Origins of First Wave Feminism*. Upper Saddle River, NJ, Prentice Hall.

Gillis, S., Howie, G., & Munford, R. eds. 2007. *Third Wave Feminism: Expanded Second Edition*. New York, Palgrave.

Nicholson, L. 1997. *The Second Wave: A Reader in Feminist Theory*. New York, Routledge.

Schneir, M. ed. 1994. *Feminism: The Essential Historical Writings*. New York, Vintage.

Chapter 2

Cudd, A. & Andreason, R., eds. 2004. *Feminist Theory*. Boston, Blackwell.

Dworkin, A. 1991. *Pornography: Men Possessing Women*. New York, Plume.

Firestone, S. 1970. *The Dialectic of Sex*. New York, William Morrow.

hooks, b. 1984. *Feminist Theory from Margin to Center*. Boston, South End Press.

Jagger, A. 1988. *Feminist Politics and Human Nature*. Lanham, MD, Rowman and Littlefield.

McCann, C., ed. 2002. *Feminist Theory Reader: Local and Global Perspectives*. New York, Routledge.

Nagl-Docekal, H. & Vester, K. 2006. *Feminist Philosophy*. Boulder, CO, Westview Press.

Ruddick, S. 1995 *Maternal Thinking: Towards a Politics of Peace*. Boston, Beacon Press.

Tong, R. 1998. *Feminist Thought: A More Comprehensive Introduction*. Boulder, CO, Westview Press.

Tong, R., Sterba, J., & Kourany, J., eds. 1998. *Feminist Philosophies*. Upper Saddle River, NJ, Prentice Hall.

Young, I. and Jaggar, A. 2000. *A Companion to Feminist Philosophy*. Boston, Blackwell.

Chapter 3

Benston, M. 1969. 'The Political Economy of Women's Liberation.' *Monthly Review* 21(4), 13–27.

Dalla Costa, M. 1972. *The Power of Women and the Subversion of the Community*. Bristol, Falling Wall Press.

MacKinnon, C. 2007. *Are Women Human?* Cambridge, MA, Belknap Press.

Mahowald, M. 1994. *Philosophy of Woman: An Anthology of Classic and Current Concepts*. Indianapolis, Hackett.

Mill, J.S. 1970 [1869]. *The Subjection of Women*. Cambridge, MA, MIT Press.

Mitchell, J. 1971. *Woman's Estate*. New York, Pantheon Books.

Wollstonecraft, M. 1988 [1792] *A Vindication of the Rights of Woman*. New York, Norton.

Woolf, V. 2004 [1929]. *A Room of One's Own*. New York, Penguin.

Chapter 4

Bartky, S. 1990. *Femininity and Domination: Studies in the Phenomenology of Oppression*. New York, Routledge.

Beauvoir, S. de. 1952. *The Second Sex*. New York, Knopf.

Friedan, B. 1963. *The Feminine Mystique*. New York, Dell.

Gilligan, C. 1982. *In a Different Voice*. Cambridge, MA, Harvard University Press.

Hartsock, N. 1983. 'The Feminist Standpoint: Developing the Ground for a Specifically Feminist Historical Materialism.' In S. Harding and M.B. Hintikka (eds.) *Discovering Reality: Feminist Perspectives on Epistemology, Metaphysics, Methodology, and Philosophy of Science*, 283–310. Boston, D. Reidel Publishing.

Held, V. 1993. *Feminist Morality*. Chicago, University of Chicago Press

Hoagland, S. 1990. *Lesbian Ethics: Toward New Values*. Palo Alto, CA, Institute of Lesbian Studies.

Jaggar, A. 1991. 'Feminist Ethics: Projects, Problems, Prospects.' In C. Card (ed.) *Feminist Ethics*. Lawrence, University Press of Kansas.

Noddings, N. 1984. *Caring: A Feminine Approach to Ethics and Moral Education*. Berkeley, University of California Press.

Tong, R. 1993. *Feminine and Feminist Ethics*. Belmont, CA, Wadsworth Publishing Company.

Young, I. 1990. *Justice and the Politics of Difference*. Princeton, NJ, Princeton University Press.

Chapter 5

Alcoff, L. 1993. 'How is Epistemology Political?' In R. Gottlieb (ed.) *Radical Philosophy: Tradition, Counter-Tradition, Politics*. Philadelphia, Temple University Press.

Baumgardner, J. & Richards, A. 2000. *Manifesta: Young Women, Feminism, and the Future*. New York, Farrar, Straus and Giroux.

Butler, J. 1990. *Gender Trouble: Feminism and the Subversion of Identity*. New York, Routledge.

Butler, J. 1993. *Bodies that Matter: On the Discursive Limits of Sex*. New York, Routledge.

Cixous, H. 1991. *The Book of Promethea*. Lincoln, University of Nebraska Press.

Code, L. 1981. 'Is the sex of the knower epistemologically significant?' *Metaphilosophy*, 12, 267–276.

Collins, P. H. 2005. *Black Sexual Politics: African Americans, Gender, and the New Racism*. New York, Routledge.

My Sistahs, www.mysistahs.org/features/hiphop.htm. Accessed September 19, 2008.

Warren, K. 1994. *Ecological Feminism*. New York, Routledge.

Wendell, S. 1996. *The Rejected Body: Feminist Philosophical Reflections on Disability*. New York: Routledge.

Winnubst, S. 2006. *Queering Freedom*. Bloomington, Indiana University Press.

Chapter 6

Ferree, M. & Tripp, A. 2006. *Global Feminism: Transnational Women's Activism, Organizing, and Human Rights*. New York, New York University Press.

Hesford, W. 2005. *Just Advocacy?: Women's Human Rights, Transnational Feminism, and the Politics of Representation*. New Brunswick, NJ, Rutgers University Press.

Lugones, M. 1987. 'Playfulness, "World"-Traveling, and Loving Perception.' *Hypatia: A Journal of Feminist Philosophy* 2(2): 3–19.

Mohanty, C. 2003. *Feminism without Borders: Decolonizing Theory, Practicing Solidarity*. Durham, NC, Duke University Press.

Okin, S. M. 2000. 'Feminism, Women's Human Rights, and Cultural Difference.' In Uma Narayan and Sandra Harding (eds.) *Decentering the Center*. Bloomington, Indiana University Press.

Scholz, S. 2008. *Political Solidarity*. University Park, PA, Penn State University Press.

Tronto, J. 2002. 'The "Nanny" Question in Feminism.' *Hypatia: A Journal of Feminist Philosophy*, 17(2), 34–51.

Chapter 7

Brownmiller, S. 1975. *Against Our Will: Men, Women and Rape*. New York, Random House Publishing.

Collins, P. H. 1990. *Black Feminist Thought: Knowledge, Consciousness, and the Politics of Empowerment.* Boston, Unwin Hyman.

Crenshaw, K. 1991. 'Mapping the Margins: Intersectionality, Identity Politics, and Violence Against Women of Color.' *Stanford Law Review*, 43, 1241–1299.

Delphy, C. 1970. *Close to Home: A Materialist Analysis of Women's Oppression.* Amherst, University of Massachusetts Press.

Irigaray, L. 1985. *This Sex Which is Not One.* Ithaca, NY, Cornell University Press.

Narayan, U. 1997. *Dislocating Cultures: Identities, Traditions, and Third World Feminism.* New York, Routledge.

Rich, A. 1995. *Of Woman Born: Motherhood as Experience and Institution.* London, Virago Press.

Walker, L. 1979. *The Battered Woman.* New York, Harper.

Index

A Beginner's Guide to Civil Liberties

Civil Liberties
Tom Head

978-1-85168-644-5
£9.99/ $14.95

Tom Head traverses the globe in order to provide a clear introduction to what civil liberties are and why they're worth defending. This handy guide offers a fascinating global history of civil liberties paired with inspiring advice on how to take an active role in their defence -- before it's too late.

"The book interweaves history, philosophy, and much-needed practical advice for activists. Passing on his perspective, Tom's also given us a good read!" **Patricia Ireland** – activist and former president of NOW, the National Organization for Women

"A thought-provoking work. If enough people read it a, his observation that 'civil liberties have historically been a hypocrite's business' will no longer ring true." **Mike Newdow** – campaigner famous for his efforts to ban the phrase "under God" in the American Pledge of Allegiance

Author and activist **TOM HEAD** serves as civil liberties guide for About.com, a division of the New York Times Company.

Browse further titles at
www.oneworld-publications.com

A Beginner's Guide to Racism

978-1-85168-543-1
£9.99/ $14.95

Provocative and intelligent reading for the newcomer and expert alike, this invaluable resource exposes the roots of racial thought and demonstrates why it has remained crucial to our everyday lives.

"Clearly and convincingly written." **David Theo Goldberg** – Director of the University of California Humanities Research Institute

"I've learned an enormous lot from Alana Lentin's book. I only regret that a guide like this was not in existence when sixty years ago I started to study that phenomenon, one of the most insidious and complex of our times." **Zygmunt Bauman** – Emeritus Professor of Sociology at the University of Leeds

ALANA LENTIN is a lecturer in sociology at the University of Sussex. She is the author of *Racism and Anti-Racism in Europe* (2004) and is a regular contributor to openDemocracy.net

A Beginner's Guide to Humanism

978-1-85168-589-9
£9.99/ $14.95

Showing how humanists make sense of the world using reason, experience, and sensitivity, Cave emphasizes that we can, and should, flourish without God. Lively, provocative, and refreshingly rant-free, this book is essential reading for all – whether atheist, agnostic, believer, or of no view – who wish better to understand what it means to be human.

"An admirable guide for all those non-religious who may wake up to the fact that they are humanists." **Sir Bernard Crick** – Emeritus Professor of Birkbeck College, University of London, and author of *Democracy: A Very Short Introduction*

"Humanism is loving, sharing and caring and above all an intelligent philosophical way to make the best of our own and our neighbours' lives. I could not commend it more." **Clare Rayner** – Broadcaster, writer and Vice President of the British Humanist Association

Writer and broadcaster Peter Cave teaches philosophy for The Open University and City University London. Author of the bestselling *Can A Robot Be Human?*, he chairs the Humanist Philosophers' Group, frequently contributes to philosophy journals and magazines, and has presented several philosophy programmes for the BBC. He lives in London.

Browse further titles at
www.oneworld-publications.com